THE BIG MUSIC QUIZ BOOK

Other musical titles by the same author

Beyond the Summertime: The Mungo Jerry story
[with Derek Wadeson]

Roy Wood: The Move, Wizzard and beyond

The little book of The Beatles

Jeff Lynne: The Electric Light Orchestra, before and after

Pop Pickers and Music Vendors: David Jacobs, Alan Freeman, John Peel, Tommy Vance and Roger Scott

A Beatles Miscellany: All you ever wanted to know but were afraid to ask

We Can Swing Together: The story of Lindisfarne

While You See a Chance: The Steve Winwood story

All Around my Hat: The Steeleye Span story

Electric Light Orchestra Song by Song

Led Zeppelin Song by Song

THE BIG MUSIC QUIZ BOOK

John Van der Kiste

A & F Publications

First published 2011 by Amazon Kindle
Revised edition published by A & F 2015
Reprinted with additional questions 2016
Second edition 2018

A & F Publications,
South Brent, Devon, England TQ10 9AS

ISBN-13: 978-1724189837

Printed by KDP

CONTENTS

INTRODUCTION

Some years ago, I was involved in producing music quizzes for a local pub. My brief was to focus largely but not exclusively on pop and rock music – in other words, a bit of something for everyone. As another nearby pub was also music quizzing and concentrating completely on pop, I decided we would make ours slightly different by including a few questions on the classics, folk, jazz, blues and all the rest in between. Nearly expects everyone to expect a music quiz to be mostly if not completely pop and rock, and there are severe limits to the number of questions you can ask on the other genres which can be answered by those who are not specialists. But that's no excuse for not being a little more inclusive.

This is what I have attempted to do in this quiz book. The two big mix rounds at either end have – well, a big mix. Expect a bit of folk, blues, jazz here and there. Elsewhere, there are tests of your knowledge on the music of each decade from the 1950s to the 1990s and another on the 21st century, alongside duets, Christmas hits, song titles containing animals, birds, numbers and the like, as well as some of the greats like the Beatles, Bowie, Springsteen, Led Zeppelin and Michael Jackson. And you will also find rounds on the classics, opera, and the musicals as well. Eclectic or what?

We called our events 'The All Music Quiz'. I did consider adopting that title for this book as well, but in view of the fact that if I did a certain well-known music website which had the title long before me might consult their lawyers, I considered again. I could have gone for 'The Best Music Quiz Book in the World...Ever!' but, once again, objections might have been raised. They can afford good lawyers. I can't.

I've refrained from dividing questions into 'easy' and 'hard'. All questions are easy – if you know the answers. If I hadn't set the questions myself, I'd have found anything relating to the last few years pretty difficult, but would breeze through those on music from three or four decades back. Age can be a terrible thing. Seriously, I have made a conscious effort to strike a balance between the simple and the more demanding. And if you want a round or two of intros, pictures and the like, sorry but you'll need to provide your own. I've done the rest, I've done my best.

Now, the serious bit. Shortly after I compiled the first (e-book only) edition, the pop music nostalgia industry was tainted somewhat with revelations about a then recently-deceased DJ and a previously much-loved entertainer. There was one question pertaining to each. On the grounds that there is a limit as to how much these things can be airbrushed out of history for their own sake no matter how distasteful, they have been left as they were. Enough said.

Unless otherwise stated, all chart positions refer to the UK charts. Singles, song, opera, film, programme and book titles are given in italics, while album titles are in inverted commas.

So whether you want to test yourself and friends or family, or whether you've promised to host a music quiz at your favourite hostelry tomorrow and have just realized you don't have enough time to set any questions of your own, I hope you've found the right thing here. And if a tie-breaker is required, you will find ten at the end. Let nobody say I don't think of everything – well, almost everything.

Thanks to Jackie for her interest and her encouragement throughout, and to Gill for a marvellous cover.

OK, waffling done. Get down to business, and enjoy these 2510 – yes, 2510 - questions. As a well-known TV quizmaster might say, your starter for ten...

The Big Mix

The majority of these should be pretty easy, but with a few more demanding ones thrown in. The vast majority are pop and rock, but look out for one or two from other genres. If this helping isn't enough, you will find another one nearer the end of the book.

1. In which year did ABBA win the Eurovision Song Contest with *Waterloo*?
2. Who was the vocalist with Simply Red?
3. Who was guitarist successively with the Yardbirds, John Mayall's Bluesbreakers, Cream, Blind Faith, and Derek and the Dominoes?
4. Which composer was born in Salzburg in 1756?
5. Which blues musician died in Chicago in 1929, reportedly from a heart attack after getting disorientated during a snowstorm?
6. Which group had a No. 1 hit with *Take My Breath Away* from the film *Top Gun* in 1986?
7. Which funky animal gave the Goodies their most successful hit?
8. Who was the guest vocalist with the Pogues on *Fairytale Of New York?*
9. Paddy Moloney plays the Uillean pipes in which folk group?
10. Which song was a hit for Carl Perkins and also for Elvis Presley in 1956?
11. At the Party at the Palace during the Golden Jubilee celebrations in June 2002, which guitarist played the National Anthem while standing on the roof of Buckingham Palace?

12. Which former member of Procol Harum went to court in 2005 to claim a share in the composing royalties for *A Whiter Shade Of Pale?*
13. Rodgers and Hammerstein's last musical opened in Broadway in 1959 and became a very successful film five years later – what was the title?
14. Which guitarist is best remembered for his hit *Guitar Boogie Shuffle* and his tutor *Play In a Day*?
15. Which music radio presenter was widely known for his catch phrases 'Not 'arf!' and 'Greetings, pop pickers'?
16. Which pop artist designed the sleeve for the Beatles' 'Sergeant Pepper's Lonely Hearts Club Band'?
17. Who did Sid Vicious replace as bassist in the Sex Pistols?
18. Which country and western singer was killed in a private plane crash in July 1964?
19. Which animal featured in the titles of No. 1 hits by Mud and Survivor?
20. What instrument is a Fender Telecaster?
21. Which surname links an Irish blues/rock guitarist, one half of a popular Scottish singer-songwriting duo in the 1970s, and brothers Noel and Liam in Oasis?
22. Can you complete the following song title by Lita Roza, *How Much Is That...*?
23. Which Plymouth-born composer and conductor wrote the *Drake 400 Suite*?
24. Which 1990s group featured the twin sisters Edele and Keavy Lynch?
25. *Fight For This Love* was the best-selling single in Britain in 2009 - who recorded it?

26. Which music hall performer turned film star was well-known for songs like *Leaning on a Lamp Post* and *My Little Stick of Blackpool Rock*?
27. John Coughlan, Peter Kircher, Jeff Rich and Matthew Letley were in turn drummers with which long-established British group?
28. Which BBC TV music show was hosted successively by Richard Williams, Bob Harris and Annie Nightingale?
29. Which magazine was founded in 1967 by Jann Wenner and Ralph Gleason?
30. Which small electronic instrument was played on *Space Oddity* by David Bowie?
31. Which jazz pianist took a very successful walk in the black forest in 1965?
32. Which comedy group from Leighton Buzzard had hits in the 1960s and 1970s parodying other artists' hits on records like *Call Up The Groups* and *Pop Go the Workers*?
33. Who had Top 10 hits in the 1960s with *Bend Me Shape Me* and *High in the Sky*?
34. Which Gilbert & Sullivan operetta has the sub-title 'The lass that loved a sailor'?
35. Which jazz singer of the 30s was known as 'The Hi De Ho Man' and whose greatest success was *Minnie the Moocher*?
36. Which writer, who died in 1985, was best known as a poet but was also a professional librarian and jazz critic?
37. How did Charlie Chaplin become Top of the Pops in 1967?
38. According to the old Irish song made famous in the 1960s by Val Doonican, who fell in for a fortune and bought himself a goat?

39. What one-word hit title do Seal, Mud, Icehouse, Patsy Cline, Aerosmith and Gnarls Barkley all have in common?
40. In which country was jazz guitarist Django Reinhardt born?
41. What was Michael Jackson's first British No. 1?
42. When Queen went on tour in 2005 and recorded a new album in 2008, which singer replaced Freddie Mercury?
43. Which singer-songwriter also wrote the novels *The Favourite Game* and *Beautiful Losers*, and books of poetry *The Spicebox of Earth* and *Flowers for Hitler*?
44. Which song was first a hit for Frank Sinatra, and subsequently for Dorothy Squires, Elvis Presley, the Sex Pistols, and Shane MacGowan?
45. How did the group Lindisfarne take their name?
46. Which musical instrument with reeds, first produced in 1821, has two main types, the chromatic and the diatonic?
47. Which American guitarist, whose career was cut short by his death after a motorcycle crash in October 1971, was sometimes known by his nickname 'Skydog'?
48. Which punk/new wave hit of the late 70s was said to be John Peel's all-time favourite record?
49. Which female singer also appeared in leading roles in the films *Mask, Moonstruck*, and *The Witches of Eastwick*?
50. Who was known as 'Father of the Blues', and whose most famous compositions are *Memphis Blues* and *St Louis Blues*?
51. Which song, written and originally recorded by Tim Moore, was covered by the Bay City

Rollers, the Records, and the Scratch Band, and was reputedly a great favourite of Keith Richards?

52. What do Sherlock Holmes and Gerry Rafferty have in common?

53. What was the name of Elvis Presley's backing group?

54. Who released the 2004 album *How To Dismantle An Atomic Bomb*?

55. *Dirty Old Town* was written by Ewan McColl about which town?

56. Who had more No 1 hits in the UK in the 90s, Take That or the Spice Girls, or did they both have the same total?

57. The Dave Clark Five had two hit records, one in 1965 and a much more successful one in 1967, which were different songs but shared what common title?

58. Which studios were established by EMI Records in 1931?

59. The Broadway musical *Jersey Boys*, which opened in 2005, is based on the story of which group?

60. Which song has been a No. 1 hit for Jimmy Young, the Righteous Brothers, Robson & Jerome, and Gareth Gates?

61. Which group played their first gig in September 1968 as the New Yardbirds?

62. With which instrument would you associate Mik Kaminski of ELO, Dave Arbus of East of Eden, and Nigel Kennedy?

63. Which top three hit from 1969 was reissued after being featured in a TV advert for lager and went to No. 1 in 1988?

64. Laurel and Hardy's *The Trail of the Lonesome Pine* came from the soundtrack of which of their films?

65. Which singer recorded the albums 'Songs For Swingin' Lovers', 'In the Wee Small Hours', and 'Come Fly With Me'?
66. In which year was the final weekly edition of *Top Of The Pops* broadcast?
67. Who had a Top 10 hit in 1973 with *You Can Do Magic*?
68. In which city is the Grand Ole Opry based?
69. In 1953 Jo Stafford was the first female vocalist to top the UK singles chart, but with which song?
70. Which ragtime pianist wrote *Maple Leaf Rag* and *The Entertainer*?
71. Jimi Hendrix, Peter Tosh and Judas Priest all had minor hits in the 1970s or 1980s with their version of which Chuck Berry classic?
72. With which instrument do you associate Benny Goodman?
73. Whose last public appearance on stage was at the Roundhouse, Camden, on 20 July 2011 with her goddaughter?
74. Which stringed instrument from the Andes belongs to the lute family, is traditionally made from the shell of the back of an armadillo, and usually has ten strings in five courses of two strings each?
75. *Love Sensation* by Loleatta Holloway was extensively sampled on which 1999 No. 1 hit?
76. Which 1960s group was initially known as the Mann-Hugg Blues Brothers?
77. *Honky Tonk Train Blues,* a hit for Keith Emerson in 1976, was written and originally recorded by whom in the 1920s?
78. Which father and daughter had a No. 1 in 2003 with the duet *Changes*?
79. Who had No. 1 albums with *Songbird, Imagine* and *American Tune* after her death?

80. The first jukebox in the world was installed at the Palais Royal Hotel in which city?
81. In festivals, what do the initials WOMAD stand for?
82. Which performer withdrew all her music from Spotify in 2014 as she was 'not willing to contribute her life's work to an experiment' that she believed did not adequately compensate writers, producers, artists, and creators for their work?
83. Which electronic music pioneers released the album 'Autobahn' in 1974?
84. Which Motown classic was performed in a pre-recorded video at Live Aid in 1985 and later released as a chart-topping single by David Bowie and Mick Jagger?
85. Which Beatles film was premiered on BBC TV on Boxing Day 1967?
86. Lena Martell topped the UK charts in 1979 with *One Day At a Time*, but who wrote it?
87. Ms Darwish was only aged sixteen when she had a No. 1 single on both sides of the Atlantic in 1987 and 1988 with a song which was a hit for Tommy James and the Shondells twenty years earlier. By what name was she better known?
88. Which blues singer was imprisoned for murdering one of his relatives but later pardoned and released, and was styled 'King of the 12-string guitar'?
89. Which Spanish dance in triple rhythm is said to have originated in Cadiz around 1780?
90. Which singer-songwriter and guitarist was a founder member of Fairport Convention until leaving in 1971 to go solo?
91. From which city did The Move and The Moody Blues come?

92. Which Russian composer first achieved international fame after composing three ballets commissioned by Sergei Diaghilev between 1910 and 1913?
93. Which Bobby Goldsboro ballad reached No. 2 in the UK in 1968 and the same position on reissue in 1975?
94. The Stephen Sondheim musical *Sunday In the Park With George* was inspired by a famous painting by which 19th century French artist?
95. *Alexander's Ragtime Band*, written around 1911, was one of the earliest songs by whom?
96. What was the full name of the American band Chicago, until legal action forced them to shorten it to the one word?
97. What was Voyager's only Top 40 hit, in 1979?
98. Which mythological place features in the titles of No. 1 hits by Dave Dee, Dozy, Beaky, Mick & Tich, and Olivia Newton-John with ELO?
99. What was the title of the Jam's live album, released at the time they disbanded in 1982?
100. Which musical, with lyrics written by Jack Good, is based loosely on Shakespeare's *Othello*?

Answers

1. 1974
2. Mick Hucknall
3. Eric Clapton
4. Wolfgang Amadeus Mozart
5. Blind Lemon Jefferson
6. Berlin
7. The gibbon
8. Kirsty MacColl

9. The Chieftains
10. *Blue Suede Shoes*
11. Brian May
12. Matthew Fisher
13. *The Sound of Music*
14. Bert Weedon
15. Alan Freeman
16. Peter Blake
17. Glen Matlock
18. Jim Reeves
19. Tiger
20. Guitar
21. Gallagher (the first two were Rory and Benny G)
22. *Doggie in the Window*
23. Ron Goodwin
24. B*witched
25. Cheryl Cole
26. George Formby
27. Status Quo
28. *The Old Grey Whistle Test*
29. *Rolling Stone*
30. Stylophone
31. Horst Jankowski
32. The Barron Knights
33. Amen Corner
34. *H.M.S. Pinafore*
35. Cab Calloway
36. Philip Larkin
37. He wrote Petula Clark's No. 1, *This Is My Song*
38. Paddy McGinty
39. *Crazy*
40. Belgium
41. *One Day In Your Life*
42. Paul Rodgers
43. Leonard Cohen

44. *My Way*
45. From the Holy Island off the north-eastern coast
46. Harmonica
47. Duane Allman
48. *Teenage Kicks*, The Undertones
49. Cher
50. W.C. Handy
51. *Rock'n'Roll Love Letter*
52. Baker Street
53. The Jordanaires
54. U2
55. Salford
56. The same – both had 8
57. *Everybody Knows*
58. Abbey Road
59. The Four Seasons
60. *Unchained Melody*
61. Led Zeppelin
62. Violin
63. *He Ain't Heavy, He's My Brother*, The Hollies
64. *Way Out West*
65. Frank Sinatra
66. 2006
67. Limmie and Family Cookin'
68. Nashville
69. *You Belong To Me*
70. Scott Joplin
71. *Johnny B. Goode*
72. Clarinet
73. Amy Winehouse
74. Charango
75. *Ride On Time,* Black Box
76. Manfred Mann
77. Meade Lux Lewis
78. Ozzy and Kelly Osbourne

79. Eva Cassidy
80. San Francisco
81. World of Music Arts and Dance
82. Taylor Swift
83. Kraftwerk
84. *Dancing In the Street*
85. *Magical Mystery Tour*
86. Kris Kristofferson
87. Tiffany. (The song was *I Think We're Alone Now)*
88. Leadbelly
89. Bolero
90. Richard Thompson
91. Birmingham
92. Igor Stravinsky
93. *Honey*
94. Georges Seurat
95. Irving Berlin
96. Chicago Transit Authority
97. Halfway Hotel
98. Xanadu
99. 'Dig the New Breed'
100. *Catch My Soul*

Once at One

The following acts all had only one UK No. 1 hit – name the hit and the year, or years. In the case of those which did so over the Christmas and new year, either will be acceptable.

1. Al Martino
2. Rednex
3. Rolf Harris
4. Kaiser Chiefs
5. T'Pau
6. Temperance Seven
7. Procol Harum
8. Dusty Springfield
9. Jamiroquai
10. Norman Greenbaum
11. Jim Diamond
12. Freda Payne
13. Another Level
14. Maria McKee
15. The Stylistics
16. Evanescence
17. Tab Hunter
18. 2 Unlimited
19. Tim McGraw
20. The Corrs

Answers

1. *Here In My Heart*, 1952-3
2. *Cotton-Eye Joe*, 1995
3. *Two Little Boys*, 1969-70

4. *Ruby,* 2007
5. *China In Your Hand*, 1987
6. *You're Driving Me Crazy*, 1961
7. *A Whiter Shade of Pale*, 1967
8. *You Don't Have To Say You Love Me*, 1966
9. *Canned Heat*, 1998
10. *Spirit In the Sky*, 1970
11. *I Should Have Known Better,* 1984
12. *Band of Gold*, 1970
13. *Freak Me*, 1998
14. *Show Me Heaven*, 1990
15. *I Can't Give You Anything But My Love*, 1975
16. *Bring Me To Life*, 2003
17. *Young Love*, 1957
18. *No Limit*, 1992
19. *Over And Over*, 2005
20. *Breathless*, 2000

Which was the year?

A famous event, and two hit records – but when did they happen?

1. President Nixon of the United States of America resigned after the Watergate scandal - *Waterloo,* ABBA - *When Will I See You Again,* Three Degrees
2. The first GM (genetically modified) products went on sale in the UK – *Killing Me Softly,* Fugees – *Breathe,* Prodigy
3. The British great train robbery took place - *I Like It,* Gerry & the Pacemakers - *From a Jack To a King,* Ned Miller
4. Great Britain and Ireland both joined the European Economic Community – *Cum On Feel the Noize,* Slade – *Welcome Home,* Peters and Lee
5. The Docklands Light Railway opened in London - *Never Gonna Give You Up,* Rick Astley - *Pump Up The Volume,* MARRS
6. Colonel Nasser seized power in Egypt – *Cara Mia,* David Whitfield - *Secret Love,* Doris Day
7. Sebastian Coe set a new record for running a mile (3 min 49 sec) – *Heart of Glass,* Blondie – *Message In A Bottle*, Police
8. *Dad's Army* was first shown on TV – *Those Were the Days,* Mary Hopkin – *Mighty Quinn,* Manfred Mann
9. Concorde made its last commercial flight – *Crazy In Love,* Beyonce - *Hole In the Head,* Sugababes

10. The House of Commons was televised for the first time – *Belfast Child,* Simple Minds - *Eternal Flame,* Bangles

11. Torrey Canyon was wrecked off the Cornish coast - *I'm a Believer,* Monkees - *Let the Heartaches Begin,* Long John Baldry

12. Harold Wilson resigned as British Prime Minister – *Save Your Kisses For Me,* Brotherhood of Man – *She,* Charles Aznavour

13. 'Black Wednesday', Britain was forced out of the European Rate Exchange mechanism – *Stay,* Shakespear's Sister – *Ebeneezer Goode,* The Shamen

14. Decimal currency was introduced in Britain – *Knock Three Times,* Dawn, *I'm Still Waiting,* Diana Ross

15. Brazil beat Sweden to win the World Cup - *Tom Dooley,* Kingston Trio - *Smoke Gets In Your Eyes,* Platters

16. Britain and China signed an agreement to return Hong Kong to China in 1997 - *Two Tribes,* Frankie Goes To Hollywood - *Hello,* Lionel Richie

17. The UK voting age was lowered from 21 to 18 – *Spirit In the Sky,* Norman Greenbaum – *Tears Of A Clown,* Smokey Robinson and the Miracles

18. The Cuban missile crisis – *Lovesick Blues,* Frank Ifield, *Telstar,* Tornados

19. The world population officially reached the figure of 6 billion for the first time - *Mambo No 5,* Louie Bega - *Baby One More Time,* Britney Spears

20. Cigarette advertising was banned on television in the UK – *You've Lost That Lovin' Feelin',* The Righteous Brothers - *The Carnival Is Over,* Seekers

Answers

1. 1974
2. 1996
3. 1963
4. 1973
5. 1987
6. 1954
7. 1979
8. 1968
9. 2003
10. 1989
11. 1967
12. 1976
13. 1992
14. 1971
15. 1958
16. 1984
17. 1970
18. 1962
19. 1999
20. 1965

Sing a Rainbow – and then some

Each colour features only once in these titles.

1. Bing Crosby – ---- *Christmas*
2. Electric Light Orchestra (ELO) – *Mr* ---- Sky
3. Elvis Costello – ---- *Shoes*
4. Jimi Hendrix Experience – ----- *Haze*
5. Lemon Pipers – ---- *Tambourine*
6. Duke Ellington – *Mood* ----
7. Christie – ----- *River*
8. Cliff Richard – *Blue Turns To* ----
9. Deep Purple – ----- *Night*
10. Elkie Brooks – ---- *Wine*
11. Coasters – *Charlie* ----
12. R.E.M. – ---- *Crush*
13. INXS – *Suicide* ----
14. Perez Prado – ---- *Pink And Apple Blossom White*
15. Jeff Beck – *Hi Ho* ---- *Lining*
16. Tommy James & the Shondells – ---- *And Clover*
17. Kenny Rogers & the First Edition – ---- *Don't Take Your Love To Town*
18. Steve Earle – ----*head Road*
19. Natalie Cole – ---- *Cadillac*
20. Puccini (opera) – *The Girl Of the* ---- *West*

Answers

1. White
2. Blue
3. Red
4. Purple
5. Green
6. Indigo
7. Yellow
8. Grey
9. Black
10. Lilac
11. Brown
12. Orange
13. Blonde
14. Cherry
15. Silver
16. Crimson
17. Ruby
18. Copper
19. Pink
20. Golden

Another place, another time

The answers to the following all feature the name of a town, city, or in one case an island. None of these are London; you will find a special round [see p 290] for questions about songs associated with the capital.

1. Where did Darts' boy come from, according to one of their hits in 1978?
2. Where was there a shoot-out as sung about by Paper Lace in 1974?
3. Where were Boney M singing about in 1977?
4. Which capital did Kenny Ball and his Jazzmen visit, in music at least, in 1962?
5. Where were Typically Tropical going on holiday in 1975?
6. Where did Freddie Mercury and Montserrat Caballe find inspiration for a duet in 1987?
7. Which Anglo-American incident of the 18th century gave The Sensational Alex Harvey Band a hit in 1976?
8. Which Olympic location proved tuneful for Helmut Zacharias in 1964?
9. Where did Katrina and the Waves, and the Bangles (same song, the latter being a cover version), go in the mid-1980s?
10. Which traditional Cornish folk song appeared on Steeleye Span's most successful album 'All Around My Hat'?
11. Where were the Mobiles in some danger in 1982?

12. Where on the south coast was Mike Oldfield in 1976?
13. Which city and which liberty did Elton John celebrate in 1975?
14. Where did Gary Moore and Phil Lynott walk in 1979?
15 Where in Europe were the Beautiful South in 1996?
16. Which city inspired hits by Michael Nesmith in 1977 and Duran Duran in 1982?
17. Where did Redbone's unwelcome character come from in 1971?
18. Where were the Four Tops hanging out in 1988?
19. Where did Siouxsie and the Banshees find somewhere exotic outdoors in 1978?
20. Which glittering resort gave Tony Christie his first hit in 1970?

Answers

1. New York City (*The Boy From New York City*)
2. Chicago (*The Night Chicago Died*)
3. *Belfast*
4. Moscow (*Midnight In Moscow*)
5. *Barbados*
6. *Barcelona*
7. *Boston Tea Party*
8. Tokyo (*Tokyo Melody*)
9. Liverpool (*Going Down To Liverpool*)
10. *Cadgwith Anthem*
11. Berlin (*Drowning in Berlin*)
12. *Portsmouth*
13. *Philadelphia Freedom*
14. Paris (*Parisienne Walkways)*
15. *Rotterdam (or Anywhere)*

16. *Rio*
17. New Orleans *(Witch Queen of New Orleans)*
18. Acapulco *(Loco in Acapulco)*
19. Hong Kong *(Hong Kong Garden)*
20. *Las Vegas*

Backing Groups

Which groups backed the following artists?

1. Billy J. Kramer
2. Brian Poole
3. Cliff Bennett
4. Bob Seger
5. Bob Marley
6. Emile Ford
7. Wayne Fontana
8. Booker T
9. Herb Alpert
10. Jimmy James
11. Tommy James
12. Joe Brown
13. Julie Driscoll
14. Graham Parker
15. Tony Sheridan
16. Steve Harley
17. Martha Reeves
18. Johnny Johnson
19. Elvis Presley
20. Katrina (Leskanich)

Answers

1. The Dakotas
2. The Tremeloes
3. The Rebel Rousers
4. The Silver Bullet Band
5. The Wailers
6. The Checkmates

7. The Mindbenders
8. The MGs
9. The Tijuana Brass
10. The Vagabonds
11. The Shondells
12. The Bruvvers
13. Brian Auger and The Trinity
14. The Rumour
15. The Beatles
16. Cockney Rebel
17. The Vandellas
18. The Bandwagon
19. The Jordanaires
20. The Waves

Singers and groups

Of which groups were the following the singers?

1. Judith Durham
2. Levi Stubbs
3. Steve Ellis
4. Clem Curtis
5. Alvin Lee
6. Ian Hunter
7. Brian Connolly
8. Gwen Dickey
9. Phil Lynott
10. Robin Zander
11. Morten Harket
12. Pete Shelley
13. Phil Oakey
14. Dave Gahan
15. Marti Pellow
16. Shane McGowan
17. Kurt Cobain
18. Damon Albarn
19. Ronan Keating
20. Mel C (Chisholm)

Answers

1. The Seekers
2. The Four Tops
3. The Love Affair (unless anybody also remembers the not very successful Widowmaker)
4. The Foundations

5. Ten Years After
6. Mott The Hoople
7. Sweet
8. Rose Royce
9. Thin Lizzy
10. Cheap Trick
11. A-Ha
12. The Buzzcocks
13. The Human League
14. Depeche Mode
15. Wet Wet Wet
16. The Pogues
17. Nirvana
18. Blur
19. Boyzone
20. Spice Girls

Real names

Under which professional names are or were the following better known?

1. Stuart Goddard
2. Richard Starkey
3. Don van Vliet
4. Stefani Germanotta
5. Marvin Lee Aday
6. Georgios Kyriacos Panayiotou
7. Reginald Kenneth Dwight
8. William Perks
9. Noah Kaminsky
10. Ernest Evans
11. Vincent Furnier
12. Marshal Bruce Mathers
13. Nathaniel Coles
14. Thomas Woodward
15. Grace Mendoza
16. Herbert Buckingham Khaury
17. Leslie Charles
18. McKinley Morganfield
19. Virginia Pugh
20. Pauline Matthews

Answers

1. Adam Ant
2. Ringo Starr
3. Captain Beefheart
4. Lady Gaga
5. Meat Loaf

6. George Michael
7. Elton John
8. Bill Wyman
9. Neil Diamond
10. Chubby Checker
11. Alice Cooper
12. Eminem
13. Nat King Cole
14. Tom Jones
15. Grace Jones
16. Tiny Tim
17. Billy Ocean
18. Muddy Waters
19. Tammy Wynette
20. Kiki Dee

What's in a Name

Identify these groups from how they chose their names.

1. A character in Charles Dickens's *David Copperfield.*
2. A novel published in 1970 by Willard Manus.
3. A milk bar drink in the movie *Clockwork Orange.*
4. A novel by Hermann Hesse.
5. A Boris Karloff classic horror film released in 1963.
6. The inventor of the seed drill.
7. A song from the first album by Leonard Cohen.
8. A clothing shop in Yorkshire.
9. A feline character in T.S. Eliot's *Old Possum's Book of Practical Cats.*
10. Dorothy's dog in *The Wizard of Oz.*
11. A Nazi slang term for a brothel.
12. A novel by John Steinbeck.
13. The Gaelic for family.
14. A headline in *Variety* magazine about Frank Sinatra moving from Las Vegas to a well-known movie location.
15. A medieval instrument of torture.
16. A song by Prince Buster.
17. A novel by John Dos Passos.
18. A film starring John Wayne, released in 1956.
19. A novel by William Burroughs.
20. The nickname of jazz musician Charlie Parker.

Answers

1. Uriah Heep
2. Mott The Hoople
3. Moloko
4. Steppenwolf
5. Black Sabbath
6. Jethro Tull
7. Sisters Of Mercy
8. Everything But The Girl
9. Mungo Jerry (albeit spelt a little differently)
10. Toto
11. Joy Division
12. East of Eden
13. Clannad
14. Frankie Goes To Hollywood
15. Iron Maiden
16. Madness
17. Manhattan Transfer
18. The Searchers
19. Soft Machine
20. The Yardbirds

Same title – different song

As there is no copyright in a song title, many titles have been used for more than one song. Can you identify the titles which gave these acts hits with different songs during particular years?

1. Sandie Shaw (1965), Olivia Newton-John (1974)
2. Ringo Starr (1973), Def Leppard (1983), Ed Sheeran (2015)
3. Slade (1974), Phil Collins (1994), Bon Jovi (2002)
4. Roxy Music (1974), U2 (1989), Bryan Adams (1992)
5. Marmalade (1970), Peters and Lee (1974)
6. Marianne Faithfull (1965), John Travolta and Olivia Newton-John (1978)
7. The Hollies (1964), Whitesnake (1982)
8. Dave Dee, Dozy, Beaky, Mick and Tich (1966), Queen (1980)
9. The Bandwagon (1969), George Harrison (1975)
10. The Pretty Things (1964), The Animals (1965), ELO (1979)
11. T. Rex (1971), David Essex (1980), Kelly Marie (1981)
12. Petula Clark (1957), Heart (1987), The Bee Gees (1997)
13. Chris Montez (1962, 1972), David Bowie (1983), Chris Rea (1987)
14. Val Doonican (1971), Wet Wet Wet (1996)

15. Petula Clark (1966), Paul McCartney and Wings (1973), Westlife (2000)
16. Faces (1972), Blue Mink (1972), Erasure (1995)
17. Elvis Presley (1960), Lionel Richie (1984)
18. The Move (1971), The Rubettes (1974), New Kids on the Block (1990)
19. Whitesnake (1981), Eurythmics (1985), Charles and Eddie (1992)
20. The Kinks (1965), Jaki Graham (1986)

Answers

1. *Long Live Love*
2. *Photograph*
3. *Everyday*
4. *All I Want Is You*
5. *Rainbow*
6. *Summer Nights*
7. *Here I Go Again*
8. *Save Me*
9. *You*
10. *Don't Bring Me Down*
11. *Hot Love*
12. *Alone*
13. *Let's Dance*
14. *Morning*
15. *My Love*
16. *Stay With Me*
17. *Stuck On You*
18. *Tonight*
19. *Would I Lie To You*
20. *Set Me Free*

The Eurovision Song Contest

Love it, hate it – but how well can you remember it?

1. In which year did four entries, including that for the UK, tie for the winning position?
2. Which country won in 1972 and 1973?
3. Which country was the winner of the first contest in 1956?
4. Britain did not enter in 1956 and in which other year?
5. Which singer won representing Switzerland in 1988, and went on to have two UK No. 1 hits in the 1990s?
6. In 2003, the UK came last for the first time with 'nul points', with which song and artist?
7. Lordi won the contest for Finland in 2006 with which song?
8. Which act represented the UK in 1979 with *Mary Ann* and came seventh, but had greater success in the mid-1980s with a series of novelty hits in the UK chart?
9. Which future *East Enders* actress represented the UK in 1991, when she came tenth?
10. Which songwriting partnership wrote the UK late 1960s entries *Puppet On a String, Congratulations* and also some of the earlier Bay City Rollers hits?
11. Mouth and MacNeal, who represented the Netherlands in 1974, reached the UK top ten

with their entry later that year – what was it called?
12. Which singer gave the UK its first win at the contest, in 1967?
13. Cliff Richard entered twice, coming second in 1968 and fourth in which other year?
14. Which duo came second for the UK in 1977 with *Rock Bottom*?
15. In 1995, the title of the act representing the UK was also the title of their entry – what was it?
16. Which successful balladeer of the late 1960s represented the UK in 2012?
17. Katrina and the Waves won the contest for the UK in 1997 with which song?
18. Cheryl Baker, later a member of Bucks Fizz, was also a member of Co-Co who sang the 1978 UK entry - what was it called?
19. In which year did Julio Iglesias represent Spain in the contest?
20. Despite less stellar performances in recent years, the UK holds the record for the highest number of runner-up placings in the contest – as of 2015, how many altogether?

Answers

1. 1969
2. Luxembourg
3. Switzerland
4. 1958
5. Celine Dion
6. *Cry Baby*, by Jemini
7. *Hard Rock Hallelujah*
8. Black Lace
9. Samantha Janus

10. Bill Martin and Phil Coulter
11. *I See a Star*
12. Sandie Shaw (with *Puppet on a String*)
13. 1973
14. Lynsey de Paul and Mike Moran
15. Love City Groove
16. Engelbert Humperdinck
17. *Love Shine a Light*
18. *The Bad Old Days*
19. 1970
20. 15

I don't hear the title

The following songs did not include the complete title (although in some cases they included one word or more from it) in the lyrics. Can you identify them?

1. A Top 10 hit for Bob Dylan in 1966, from the album 'Blonde on Blonde'.
2. The only hit for Keith West, in 1967.
3. The last Beatles' UK No. 1, in 1969.
4. The first Top 10 hit for David Bowie, in 1969, and a No. 1 on reissue in 1975.
5. A hit three times over for New Order, in 1983, 1988 and 1995.
6. A hit for Rod Stewart in 1981.
7. A No. 1 hit for Queen in 1975-6 and in 1991-2.
8. The first hit for Wizzard, in 1972-3.
9. The last hit for Cream, in 1969.
10. The first hit for the Bee Gees, in 1967.
11. The first hit for ELO, in 1972.
12. Robert Plant's most successful single in 1983.
13. A Top 10 hit for Black Sabbath in 1970 and a Top 20 reissue ten years later.
14. The first hit for Kiki Dee, in 1973.
15. Rush's only Top 20 single, in 1980.
16. Donovan's most successful single, in 1966.
17. An autobiographical Top 10 hit for The Mamas and the Papas in 1967.
18. A Top 10 hit for Gorillaz in 2005.
19. The Toys' only Top 10 hit, in 1965.
20. A hit for the Monkees in 1967, the original title of which had to be changed in order not to cause offence – though more recent issues on CD have

reverted to the group's initial choice. (Have a bonus point if you can name both).

Answers

1. *Rainy Day Women #12 & 35*
2. *Excerpt From a Teenage Opera*
3. *The Ballad of John and Yoko*
4. *Space Oddity*
5. *Blue Monday*
6. *Young Turks*
7. *Bohemian Rhapsody*
8. *Ball Park Incident*
9. *Badge*
10. *New York Mining Disaster 1941*
11. *10538 Overture*
12. *Big Log*
13. *Paranoid*
14. *Amoreuse*
15. *The Spirit of Radio*
16. *Sunshine Superman*
17. *Creeque Alley*
18. *Dirty Harry*
19. *A Lover's Concerto*
20. *Alternate Title* (the title under which it was first released and became a hit); *Randy Scouse Git* (the group's original title)

DJs On Record

Not content with playing the records on air, some attempted a brief shot at stardom with making one or two themselves, while one had already had a pretty good track, er, record already.

1. Which group backed Jimmy Savile on his 1962 single *Ahab the Arab*?
2. Noel Edmonds was part of which group who charted in 1981 with *I Wanna Be a Winner*?
3. Dave Lee Travis and Paul Burnett had a hit in 1976 with *Convoy GB* under what name?
4. What was the title of Alan Freeman's 1962 dance single?
5. Who had a Top 10 hit in 1982 with *Snot Rap*?
6. Who had a brief spoken part on Lynsey De Paul's *Won't Somebody Dance With Me*?
7. John Peel can be heard on backing vocals on Neil Diamond's *Song Sung Blue*, as covered by which group in 1982?
8. On which 1991 Top 30 hit did Mike Read have a short voice-over?
9. A Northern soul single in 1973 was issued by Tony Blackburn under what alias?
10. Which Radio 2 blues programme presenter was best known in the 1960s as vocalist with a group who had two No. 1 hits, and then as an actor?
11. Which BBC radio DJ, TV presenter and talk show host released a single in 1969 called *Julie*?
12. Mike Read released the single *High Rise* in 1979 under which group name?

13. Which song did The Wurzels and Tony Blackburn release in 2007, with royalties going to the Prostate Cancer Care Appeal in Bristol?
14. Which future Radio 1 and Capital DJ released a cover version of the Rolling Stones' *Off the Hook* as a single in 1966?
15. The 1969 novelty hit *Groovy Baby* by Microbe was a spin-off from which then Radio 1 DJ's daily show?
16. In the 1980s, which Radio 1 DJ was responsible for the singles *I'm Alright, Get Some Therapy,* and *The Gay Cavalieros*?
17. In 1968 Ed Stewart was the main performer on a cover version of the Idle Race's *I Like My Toys,* but what was the artist billing on the label?
18. Which future Radio 1 and Radio 2 presenter had a No. 1 in 1955 with *The Man From Laramie*?
19. *Goodness Gracious Me,* a hit for Peter Sellers and Sophia Loren, was covered by Linda Joyce and Matt Bryant on the Embassy label. These were aliases for Maureen Grant and which BBC radio DJ (and the name Matt Bryant is a clue)?
20. As presenter of the Saturday Rock Show, Alan Freeman gave his name in 1976 to a heavy and progressive compilation album on the Atlantic label, but what was the title?

Answers

1. The Tremeloes
2. Brown Sauce
3. Laurie Lingo & The Dipsticks
4. *It's Madison Time*
5. Kenny Everett

6. Ed Stewart
7. Altered Images
8. *Radio Wall of Sound,* Slade
9. Lenny Gamble
10. Paul Jones
11. Simon Dee
12. The Trainspotters
13. *I Am a Cider Drinker*
14. Tommy Vance
15. Dave Cash
16. Steve Wright
17. Stewpot and Save The Children Fund Choir
18. Jimmy Young
19. Brian Matthew
20. 'By Invitation Only'

Comedy records

They're not all everybody's idea of a laugh – but somebody liked them. How many of these can you or will you own up to remembering, let alone being able to answer questions about them?

1. Who had a hit with *Disco Duck* in 1976?
2. What was the real name of Napoleon XIV, the *They're Coming To Take Me Away Ha-Haa!* one-hit wonder of 1966?
3. Which comedian had a minor Top 50 hit in 1973 inspired by his catchphrase 'Ooh, you are awful – but I like you!'?
4. Under which pseudonym did Paul McCartney produce the Bonzo Dog Band's *I'm the Urban Spaceman* in 1968?
5. According to Ray Stevens, who was the Queen of the Blues in 1971?
6. Which dance routine song from *The Rocky Horror Picture Show* gave Damian a Top 10 hit in 1989?
7. *Axel F* was a hit for Harold Faltermeyer in 1985, but who (or what) took it to No. 1 in 2005?
8. Which comedian's only hit single was in 1961 with *Don't Jump Off the Roof Dad*?
9. Which less than glamorous duo had a Top 30 hit in 1978 with a parody of *You're the One That I Want*?
10. With which comedy team did Cliff Richard top the charts in 1986 with a spoof version of *Livin' Doll*?

11. Which comedy actor, perhaps best remembered for an appearance in one episode of *Fawlty Towers*, had Top 10 singles in 1962 with *Right Said Fred* and *Hole in the Ground*?
12. *Jilted John* was the only hit for Jilted John – but what was his real name?
13. Which question took Alexei Sayle into the Top 20 in 1984?
14. Who had hits in the 1960s with *Gather in the Mushrooms* and *Harvest of Love*?
15. *Ying Tong Song* was a Top 10 hit twice, seventeen years apart, for the Goons, but which of them wrote it?
16. Monty Python's *Always Look on the Bright Side of Life* was released as a single without success in 1979 and 1988; in which year did it finally reach the top three?
17. Who reached No. 1 in 1987 with *Star Trekkin'*?
18. Who provided the vocals on *Chocolate Salty Balls* by Chef, No. 1 in 1998?
19. Which single by the Simpsons topped the UK chart in 1991?
20. *The Bucket of Water Song* by The Four Bucketeers, a Top 30 hit in 1980, was a spin-off from which children's TV series?

Answers

1. Rick Dees and his Cast of Idiots
2. Jerry Samuels
3. Dick Emery
4. Apollo C. Vermouth. (Some sources say Gus Dudgeon co-produced with McCartney)
5. *Bridget The Midget*
6. *Time Warp*

7. Crazy Frog
8. Tommy Cooper
9. Hylda Baker and Arthur Mullard
10. The Young Ones
11. Bernard Cribbins
12. Graham Fellows
13. *Ullo John! Gotta New Motor?*
14. Benny Hill
15. Spike Milligan
16. 1991
17. The Firm
18. Isaac Hayes
19. *Do the Bartman*
20. *Tiswas*

Numbers

Can you complete these song titles with a number, or in one case, two? (For a bonus point, or several, if you're feeling mathematically bold, then add up the total). Two questions do have the same answer, by the way.

1. Marvin Gaye and Kim Weston, *It Takes ----*
2. Dusty Springfield, *I Close My Eyes and Count To ----*
3. The Stranglers, ---- *Minutes*
4. Nena, ---- *Red Balloons*
5. Robert Plant, ---- *Palms*
6. The Proclaimers, ---- *Miles*
7. Alarm,---- *Guns*
8. Status Quo, ---- *Wild Horses*
9. The Beatles, *When I'm ----*
10. Pete Wingfield, ---- *With a Bullet*
11. The Pretenders, ---- *Miles*
12. Dawn, *Knock ---- Times*
13. The Rolling Stones, *----th Nervous Breakdown*
14. Edwin Starr, ---- *Miles*
15. Sheena Easton, ---- *To* ---- [two numbers required]
16. Gary U.S. Bonds, *Quarter To ----*
17. The Four Tops, ---- *Rooms of Gloom*
18. The Eagles, ---- *of These Nights*
19. Bob Dylan, *Highway ---- Revisited*
20. The King Brothers, ---- *Trombones*

Answers

1. 2
2. 10
3. 5
4. 99
5. 29
6. 500
7. 68
8. 20
9. 64
10. 18
11. 2000
12. 3
13. 19
14. 25
15. 9 and 5
16. 3
17. 7
18. 1
19. 61
20. 76

Total – 3024

Christmas records

Which artists had hits with the following Yuletide goodies (or substitute your own less than complimentary noun)? As several have made the charts more than once, and as some have been hits for more than one artist but several years apart, the year given in which they first charted is significant.

1. *Merry Xmas Everybody*, 1973
2. *Lonely This Christmas*, 1974
3. *Last Christmas*, 1984
4. *Merry Christmas Everyone*, 1985
5. *Driving Home For Christmas*, 1986
6. *Mistletoe And Wine*, 1988
7. *Thank God It's Christmas*, 1984
8. *I Wish It Could Be Christmas Everyday*, 1973
9. *Christmas Alphabet*, 1955
10. *Christmas Time (Don't Let the Bells End)*, 2003
11. *Step Into Christmas*, 1973
12. *All I Want For Christmas Is You*, 1994
13. *A Merry Jingle*, 1979
14. *Mary's Boy Child*, 1957
15. *It's Gonna Be a Cold, Cold Christmas*, 1975
16. *Christmas Through Your Eyes*, 1992
17. *Please Come Home For Christmas*, 1994
18. *Christmas Rappin'*, 1979
19. *Christmas Wrapping*, 1982
20. *Christmas Will Be Just Another Lonely Day*, 1964

Answers

1. Slade
2. Mud
3. Wham!
4. Shakin' Stevens
5. Chris Rea
6. Cliff Richard
7. Queen
8. Wizzard
9. Dickie Valentine
10. The Darkness
11. Elton John
12. Mariah Carey
13. The Greedies
14. Harry Belafonte
15. Dana
16. Gloria Estefan
17. Bon Jovi
18. Kurtis Blow
19. The Waitresses
20. Brenda Lee

James Bond film themes

Who sang the following themes? Note – in some cases, the title of the song is not necessarily the same as the film in which it appears, in which case both titles are given.
Their chart success, or lack of it, was very varied in each case. For a bonus point, can you identify which was the only one to make No. 1 in the US chart? It proved the most successful single of the batch in the UK as well, peaking at No. 2.

1. *The Living Daylights*
2. *For Your Eyes Only*
3. *Licence To Kill*
4. *Moonraker*
5. *Thunderball*
6. *The Man With The Golden Gun*
7. *You Only Live Twice*
8. *Live And Let Die*
9. *You Know My Name* (film, *Casino Royale*)
10. *GoldenEye*
11. *A View To a Kill*
12. *Another Way To Die* (film, *Quantum of Solace*)
13. *Skyfall*
14. *From Russia With Love*
15. *Nobody Does It Better* (film, *The Spy Who Loved Me*)
16. *Goldfinger*
17. *Die Another Day*
18. *The World Is Not Enough*

19. *All Time High* (film, *Octopussy*)
20. *Tomorrow Never Dies*

Answers

1. A-ha
2. Sheena Easton
3. Gladys Knight
4. Shirley Bassey
5. Tom Jones
6. Lulu
7. Nancy Sinatra
8. Paul McCartney and Wings
9. Chris Cornell
10. Tina Turner
11. Duran Duran (No. 1 in the US)
12. Jack White and Alicia Keys
13. Adele
14. Matt Monro
15. Carly Simon
16. Shirley Bassey
17. Madonna
18. Garbage
19. Rita Coolidge
20. Sheryl Crow

Top Of The Pops

Our regular must-see on TV nearly every week from 1964 to 2006.

1. For the first two years or so, the show was initially broadcast from the Dickenson Road Studios, in which city?
2. Which model was the regular disc girl on the show until 1967?
3. Which Radio 1 disc jockey, who became a regular presenter of the programme in 1982, was seen miming mandolin to *Maggie May* by Rod Stewart and The Faces?
4. Who led the *Top Of The Pops* orchestra until it was dispensed with in the early 1980s?
5. When David Jacobs became the first of the regular presenters to step down, who replaced him?
6. On a performance in 1988, Julianne Regan of All About Eve stood silent instead of miming as she could not hear the song although the audience could; by way of apology they were invited back next week to perform live, but which was the song?
7. Pan's People were first seen dancing on the show in 1968 to *Simon Says*, a hit for which group?
8. *Yellow Pearl*, the theme between 1981 and 1986, was co-written by Phil Lynott with whom?
9. Which group made a record 106 performances on the show?
10. Which Secretary of State for Culture called for the programme to be reinstated in 2008?

11. Which group appeared on the programme on Elvis Presley's 40th birthday, 8 January 1975, and ended their performance of what was the current No. 1 with the spoken line, 'Happy birthday Elvis, wherever you are?'
12. Which darts player's picture was displayed behind a performance from Kevin Rowland and Dexy's Midnight Runners in 1982, some say as a joke, others as a genuine mistake?
13. Which Barron Knights' hit from December 1979 was removed from the 2014 run of repeats, because their parody of Chinese takeaways was considered politically incorrect?
14. Who originally devised the show and was the producer until 1973?
15. When the show was moved to BBC2 in July 2005, on which evening of the week was it transmitted?
16. In which year was the 1000th episode shown?
17. On the final show, what was the No. 1 single?
18. When he was co-presenting the programme in June 1983 on the eve of the British general election, John Peel announced that one particular video had been made in a country that still had a steel industry. Which was the record it accompanied?
19. In 1970, John Lennon and the Plastic Ono Band appeared live (or miming) in the studio, while Yoko Ono sat knitting, to which record?
20. Which group, who topped the charts in January 1982, performed both sides of their double A-side on the show one week?

Answers

1. Manchester
2. Samantha Juste (Denise Sampey was the first, but only for the first few editions)
3. John Peel
4. Johnny Pearson
5. Simon Dee
6. *Martha's Harbour*
7. The 1910 Fruitgum Co
8. Midge Ure
9. Status Quo
10. Andy Burnham
11. Mud (with *Lonely this Christmas*)
12. Jocky Wilson (the song being performed was *Jackie Wilson Says*)
13. *Food for Thought*
14. Johnnie Stewart
15. Sunday
16. 1983
17. *Hips Don't Lie*, Shakira
18. *Flashdance (What a Feeling)*, Irene Cara
19. *Instant Karma!*
20. The Jam (*A Town Called Malice, Precious*)

Artists with own record labels

The Beatles and the Rolling Stones led, and others followed, or in one or two cases had got there long before them. But which acts formed the following labels?

1. Swan Song
2. Blackened
3. Big Brother
4. A & M
5. Go-Feet
6. Roc Nation
7. Grand Royal
8. NPG
9. Threshold
10. Zarjazz
11. Reprise
12. Rocket
13. Grunt
14. Numa
15. Brother
16. Bamboo
17. Shady
18. Jeremiah
19. Satellite
20. Respond

Answers

1. Led Zeppelin
2. Metallica
3. Oasis
4. Herb Alpert (with executive Jerry Moss)
5. The Beat
6. Jay Z
7. The Beastie Boys
8. Prince (or The Artist Formerly Known as Prince)
9. The Moody Blues
10. Madness
11. Frank Sinatra
12. Elton John
13. Jefferson Starship
14. Gary Numan
15. The Beach Boys
16. Gene Chandler
17. Eminem
18. Hoyt Axton
19. Ray Dorset (Mungo Jerry)
20. Paul Weller

Politics

The following all have a political theme of sorts.

1. Which Prime Minister is mentioned in the lyrics of Elvis Costello's *Oliver's Army* and Jona Lewie's *Stop the Cavalry*?
2. Tony Blair once said that if he could sing like which particular rock vocalist, he might never have entered politics?
3. Who had a hit with *Stand Down Margaret* in 1980?
4. Peter Wishart, formerly a member of Big Country and Runrig, was first elected as a Scottish MP in 2001, but for which party?
5. A former MP for Plymouth Sutton and junior minister in Margaret Thatcher's government had the same name as the keyboard player with Dire Straits (spelt identically), and as the Hollies' lead singer (spelt a little differently) – but what was the name?
6. Which Victorian Prime Minister is mentioned in the title of a 1967 album by Cream?
7. Who did The Special AKA wish to free in their hit of 1984?
8. The Manic Street Preachers' *The Masses Against the Classes* took its title from a speech by which Victorian Prime Minister?
9. What was the name of the band formed by Tony Blair during his student days?
10. Prime Ministers Harold Wilson and Edward Heath were mentioned in the lyrics of which 1966 Beatles album track?

11. Which Motown singer appeared alongside Paul Weller as part of the Council Collective on the 1984 single *Soul Deep*, to raise money for the families of striking miners?
12. Who wrote the song *Ohio*, in response to the Kent State shootings on 4 May 1970?
13. Which two world leaders were namechecked in the lyrics to *Killer Queen* by Queen?
14. In which Beatles' song did John Lennon sing, 'But if you go carrying pictures of Chairman Mao, you ain't gonna make it with anyone anyhow'?
15. Stevie Wonder's 1981 hit *Happy Birthday* was part of a campaign to have the birthday of which figure recognised as a national holiday in the US?
16. At the 1998 BRIT awards, a member of which group poured a jug of water over Deputy Prime Minister John Prescott as a protest at the government's refusal to support the Liverpool dockers' strike?
17. Indie band The Family Cat demonised which Conservative minister of the time in the song *Bring Me the Head of* ---- ---- on a Top 50 EP released in 1994?
18. With which film star, later Princess of Monaco, did Bing Crosby due on the 1956 hit version of *True Love*?
19. Which record by the Blow Monkeys was banned in 1987 by Radio 1 because of its overtly political nature and its timing so close to the general election?
20. Can you supply the missing name from this lyric, taken from the Rolling Stones' *Sympathy for the Devil*: 'I shouted out, who killed the ---s, well after all, it was you and me'.

Answers

1. Winston Churchill
2. Paul Rodgers, of Free and Bad Company
3. The Beat
4. Scottish Nationalist Party
5. Alan Clark (Allan Clarke, in the case of The Hollies)
6. Disraeli ('Disraeli Gears')
7. Nelson Mandela
8. W.E. Gladstone
9. Ugly Rumours
10. *Taxman* (from 'Revolver')
11. Jimmy Ruffin
12. Neil Young
13. Khrushchev and Kennedy
14. *Revolution*
15. Martin Luther King
16. Chumbawumba
17. Michael Portillo
18. Grace Kelly
19. *Celebrate (The Day After You)*
20. Kennedy

Seasons

Who had hits with the following seasonal songs? Again, the year is significant, as some of these titles were used more than once, and in a few cases there was more than one version. And yes, it's noticeable that spring seems to inspire remarkably few songwriters – or do people simply not like buying records about spring?

1. *Summerlove Sensation*, 1974
2. *In The Summertime*, 1970
3. *Cruel Summer*, 1984
4. *Summertime City*, 1975
5. *Summer of '69*, 1985
6. *Summer Night City*, 1978
7. *The Boys of Summer*, 1985
8. *Summer Nights*, 1965
9. *Here Comes Summer*, 1959
10. *Here Comes the Summer*, 1979
11. *Long Hot Summer*, 1983
12. *Summer Breeze*, 1974
13. *Forever Autumn*, 1978
14. *Autumn Almanac*, 1967
15. *Winter World of Love*, 1969
16. *A Hazy Shade of Winter*, 1988
17. *Rock'n'Roll Winter*, 1974
18. *Warm This Winter*, 2008
19. *A Winter's Tale*, 1982
20. *Winter Melody*, 1977

Answers

1. The Bay City Rollers
2. Mungo Jerry
3. Bananarama
4. Mike Batt and the New Edition
5. Bryan Adams
6. ABBA
7. Don Henley
8. Marianne Faithfull
9. Jerry Keller
10. The Undertones
11. The Style Council
12. The Isley Brothers
13. Justin Hayward
14. The Kinks
15. Engelbert Humperdinck
16. The Bangles
17. Wizzard
18. Gabrielle Cilmi
19. David Essex
20. Donna Summer

Good and bad weather

Can you identify the following meteorologically-connected songs from the clues?

1. A soul classic and minor hit by Ann Peebles from 1973, and later a bigger hit for Eruption.
2. A song originally recorded in the 1950s and 1960s firstly by Johnny Mathis, then Nina Simone, and in the 1970s by David Bowie, the latter's version becoming a Top 30 hit for him in 1981.
3. The title song of Lindisfarne's second and most successful album in 1971, re-recorded by them and Gazza under a slightly different title as a single in 1990.
4. An apocalyptic song from Bob Dylan's second album in 1963 which ten years later became Bryan Ferry's first solo hit.
5. A 1981 top five hit for Toyah, promoted with a video by Godley and Crème.
6. The Kinks' third UK No. 1, in 1966, which later gave its name to a West End musical based on the group's career.
7. A summer feelgood anthem, celebrating the end of the rain, and 1972 Top 10 hit for Johnny Nash.
8. A track from The Move's debut album in 1968, featuring Roy Wood and a string quartet.
9. An eight-minute album track by Neil Young, from the 1977 album 'American Stars'n'Bars', and a staple of his live gigs ever since.
10. A Bee Gees song covered unsuccessfully as a 1968 single by Paul Jones, with Jeff Beck on guitar and Paul McCartney on drums.

11. The third of the Rolling Stones' UK No. 1s in 1965, described by Mick Jagger as a 'stop-bugging-me, post-teenage-alienation' song.
12. A Buddy Holly song which became a UK Top 30 hit for Leo Sayer in 1978.
13. A Stevie Wonder song written specially for The Supremes, and a Top 40 UK hit in 1973.
14. A Top 50 hit in 1989 for Enya about severe conditions in the tropics.
15. A song of gloom which topped the UK chart for the Walker Brothers in 1966.
16. A Top 10 hit in 1999 for Travis which suggests somebody needs an umbrella.
17. A UK No. 1 in 1963 for Frank Ifield, which had also previously made the Top 10 in 1956 for Gogi Grant and Tex Ritter, and the Top 30 that year for Jimmy Young.
18. A UK Top 30 hit in 1977 for Leo Sayer, whch gave him a No. 1 in 2006 after being remixed.
19. A US No. 1 and UK No. 11 in 1966 for Lou Christie.
20. A UK Top 10 hit in 1977 for Elkie Brooks looking forward to better weather.

Answers

1. *I Can't Stand the Rain*
2. *Wild is the Wind*
3. *Fog On the Tyne*
4. *A Hard Rain's a-Gonna Fall*
5. *Thunder In the Mountains*
6. *Sunny Afternoon*
7. *I Can See Clearly Now*
8. *Mist on a Monday Morning*
9. *Like a Hurricane*
10. *And the Sun Will Shine*

11. *Get Off Of My Cloud*
12. *Raining In My Heart*
13. *Bad Weather*
14. *Storms in Africa (Part II)*
15. *The Sun Ain't Gonna Shine Anymore*
16. *Why Does It Always Rain On Me?*
17. *The Wayward Wind*
18. *Thunder In My Heart* (the remix being *Thunder In My Heart Again*)
19. *Lightnin' Strikes*
20. *Sunshine After the Rain*

It's for you-hoo!

How is your knowledge of songs inspired by the telephone?

1. Who paid tribute to the inventor of the telephone in 1971 with *Alexander Graham Bell*?
2. What was the title of Blondie's second 1978 UK top five success?
3. Which Chuck Berry song opens with the words: 'Long distance information, get me…'?
4. What was the number which comprised the title of a 1966 hit for Wilson Pickett?
5. Although it had been recorded about a year previously, what was ABBA's follow-up UK hit to *Waterloo*?
6. Who reached the UK Top 10 in 1977 with *Telephone Line*, and the Top 30 in 1986 with *Calling America*?
7. Which song gave Sheena Easton a US Top 10 hit in 1983, although it only just made the UK Top 100?
8. Who had a UK Top 10 hit in 1977 when she serenaded the *Telephone Man*?
9. Which song about a telephone drama provided Dr Hook with their first UK hit in 1972?
10. Which song gave Maroon 5 featuring Wiz Khalifa a UK No. 1 in 2012?
11. What was the telephone-themed opening track on The Beatles' 'Beatles For Sale'?
12. Which song was a 1962 US hit for The Orlons, and given a new lease of life when it was featured in the 1993 movie *Dennis the Menace*?

13. Which Monkees 1966 hit tells of a man urging his partner to meet him at the station before he says goodbye, perhaps for ever?
14. Which 'connected' number gave Milli Vanilli a US No. 1 and UK Top 20 hit in 1989?
15. Who had a transatlantic No. 1 in 2012 with *Call Me Maybe*?
16. Which was the opening track from The Kinks' 1966 album 'Face to Face'?
17. What was the B-side of The Rolling Stones' *Little Red Rooster*?
18. A track from Tom Waits' 1987 album 'Franks Wild Years' is called *Telephone Call From* – where?
19. *Girl on the Phone* is a track from which album by The Jam?
20. *She May Call You Up Tonight* was one of the less successful follow-ups in 1967 to *Walk Away Renee* by which American group?

Answers

1. The Sweet
2. *Hanging On the Telephone*
3. *Memphis Tennessee*
4. *634-5789*
5. *Ring Ring*
6. ELO
7. *Telefone (Long Distance Love Affair)*
8. Meri Wilson
9. *Sylvia's Mother*
10. *Payphone*
11. *No Reply*
12. *Don't Hang Up*
13. *Last Train to Clarksville*
14. *Baby Don't Forget My Number*
15. Carly Rae Jepsen

16. *Party Line*
17. *Off the Hook*
18. Istanbul
19. 'Setting Sons'
20. The Left Banke

Ghosts, devils, spirits, magic and the rest

Fancy something for Hallowe'en? The following clues are all to songs with some supernatural element.

1. A song by R. Dean Taylor, first released in 1967 and a Top 10 hit in the UK in 1974, and subsequently a Top 30 hit for The Fall in 1987.
2. A US Top 10 and UK Top 20 hit in 1979 by the Charlie Daniels Band.
3. The Specials' second and last UK No. 1, in the summer of 1981.
4. A top three single and album title track for Queen in 1986.
5. A novelty spook song by Bobby 'Boris' Pickett and the Crypt-Kickers, a US No. 1 in 1962, banned by BBC radio at the time, but reissued to become a (no longer banned) top three UK hit eleven years later.
6. A UK top three hit for Japan in 1982, and in fact their most successful ever.
7. A Top 30 US hit for Warren Zevon, though not a hit in the UK, which featured John McVie and Mick Fleetwood on bass and drums.
8. The second and last UK No. 1 for Suzi Quatro.
9. One side of a double A-side and top three UK hit for Annie Lennox in 1993.
10. A movie theme and No. 2 UK hit in 1984 for Ray Parker Jr in 1984.
11. A No. 2 UK hit for Redbone in 1971.
12. A spookily romantic title which gave Tavares a UK Top 30 hit in 1978.

13. Billy Fury's last-ever UK hit, albeit only just reaching the Top 60, a few weeks before his death in 1983.
14. The title track of a UK Top 30 album for Bruce Springsteen in 1995.
15. A No. 3 UK hit in 1973 for Limmie and the Family Cookin'.
16. The only UK Top 10 hit, in 1971, for Atomic Rooster.
17. A monster (well, Top 20 anyway) UK hit, in fact the only UK hit, in 1973 for the Edgar Winter Group.
18. A UK No. 1 in 1963 (his 13th) and a No. 2 on reissue in 2005 for Elvis Presley, despite having been voted a 'Miss' on TV's *Juke Box Jury* by John Lennon on release.
19. The title track of a UK No. 1 album in 1979 for The Bee Gees, and a Top 20 single the following year.
20. A UK Top 10 hit in 1966 for Alan Price, which also reached the Top 20 in 1993 for Bryan Ferry and the Top 30 in 1965 for Nina Simone.

Answers

1. *There's a Ghost In My House*
2. *The Devil Came Down To Georgia*
3. *Ghost Town*
4. *A Kind of Magic*
5. *Monster Mash*
6. *Ghosts*
7. *Werewolves of London*
8. *Devil Gate Drive*
9. *Love Song For a Vampire*
10. *Ghostbusters*
11. *Witch Queen of New Orleans*
12. *The Ghost of Love*

13. *Devil or Angel*
14. *The Ghost of Tom Joad*
15. *You Can Do Magic*
16. *Devil's Answer*
17. *Frankenstein*
18. *(You're the) Devil In Disguise*
19. *Spirits Having Flown*
20. *I Put a Spell on You*

Rockin' with the Bard

Even William Shakespeare's influence can be found in popular music. All these questions have a Bard of Avon connection.

1. Who had a UK Top 10 hit in 1981 with *Romeo and Juliet*?
2. Who released the Shakespeare-themed album 'As You Like It' in 2005?
3. Who was the lead vocalist of Europe, of *The Final Countdown* fame?
4. Lear is referred to in the second verse of which Beatles hit?
5. Petula Clark had a UK No. 1 in 1961, and Mr Big a Top 10 hit in 1977, both named after which Shakespearean hero?
6. Which B.A. Robertson UK hit from 1980 takes its title from a quotation from *Hamlet*?
7. Who had a UK Top 5 hit in 1962 with *As You Like It*?
8. Which Shakespearean play shares its title with a 1982 hit by David Essex and a 1995 hit by Queen?
9. Which very successful mid-60s husband and wife duo initially recorded under the name of Caesar and Cleo?
10. Which 11-minute epic by Bob Dylan, from his 1965 album 'Highway 61 Revisited', contains the following lyrics: "And in comes Romeo, he's moaning 'You belong to me I believe'" and "Ophelia, she's 'neath the window, for her I feel so afraid"?
11. Which Mumford & Sons song takes its title from a line in *Much Ado About Nothing*?

12. Who released the live double album, 'All The World's a Stage', in 1976?
13. Which 1988 hit by Iron Maiden takes its name from a line in *Julius Caesar*?
14. Who topped the UK charts for eight weeks in 1992 with *Stay*?
15. Which Eagles US Top 40 hit includes the lines "Old Billy was right, let's kill all the lawyers – kill 'em tonight", referencing a line from *Henry VI, Part II*?
16. Which Beatles recording features a sound collage that includes a few seconds of a radio broadcast of *King Lear*?
17. Which Shakespearean character was also the name of a US Top 30 Dean Friedman hit?
18. 'Full fathom five', from *The Tempest*, is the opening line of the spoken passage which begins which Dave Dee, Dozy, Beaky, Mick & Tich hit from 1968?
19. "No man's a jester playing Shakespeare" is a line from which track on Elton John's eponymous 1970 album?
20. "As merry as the day were long" is a slight variation from a line in *Much Ado About Nothing*, the opening line of which album track by The Smiths?

Answers

1. Dire Straits
2. Barenaked Ladies
3. Joey Tempest
4. *Paperback Writer*
5. Romeo
6. *To Be or Not To Be*
7. Adam Faith

8. *A Winter's Tale*
9. Sonny and Cher
10. *Desolation Row*
11. *Sigh no More*
12. Rush
13. *The Evil That Men Do*
14. Shakespear's Sister
15. *Get Over It*
16. *I Am the Walrus*
17. *Ariel*
18. *The Wreck of the Antoinette*
19. *The King Must Die*
20. *You've Got Everything Now*

Animals and birds

Can you fill in the missing word?

1. Cat Stevens, *I Love My ----*
2. Dave and Ansell Collins, ---- *Spanner*
3. The Beatles, *I Am the ----*
4. Partners In Kryme, ---- *Power*
5. Mud, *The ---- Crept In*
6. Sweet, or Manfred Mann (different songs), --- *On the Run*
7. Michael Jackson, *Rockin' ----*
8. T. Rex, *Ride a White ----*
9. Paul Anka, or Donny Osmond, ---- *Love*
10. Gerry Rafferty, *Night ----*
11. Manfred Mann, *Pretty ----*
12. Madness, *Wings Of a ----*
13. The Tokens, or Tight Fit, *The ---- Sleeps Tonight*
14. The Steve Miller Band, *Fly Like an ----*
15. Slade, *Gypsy Road ----*
16 Kid Creole and the Coconuts, *Stool ----*
17. Bob Dylan, ---- *Skin Pill Box Hat*
18. Bob Marley and the Wailers, ---- *Soldier*
19. Little Eva, *Let's ---- Trot*
20. Everly Brothers, *On the Wings of a ----*

Answers

1. Dog
2. Monkey
3. Walrus
4. Turtle

5. Cat
6. Fox
7. Robin
8. Swan
9. Puppy
10. Owl
11. Flamingo
12. Dove
13. Lion
14. Eagle
15. Hog
16. Pigeon
17. Leopard
18. Buffalo
19. Turkey
20. Nightingale

Rock'n'Roll

The genre that really started modern music in the mid-1950s.

1. Danny and the Juniors had a transatlantic hit in 1958 with *At the Hop,* but what was Danny's full name?
2. Ringo Starr had a Top 10 hit with which song that was originally a success for Johnny Burnette?
3. Who had a US No. 1 in 1957 with *Party Doll?*
4. What was Frankie Lymon and the Teenagers' biggest hit, and also a Top 10 single many years later for Diana Ross?
5. *Shake Rattle and Roll,* a Top 10 hit early in 1955, was the first UK chart entry for which act?
6. Frederick Heath fronted the Pirates, but by what name was he better known?
7. *Schoolboy Crush* was originally the A-side of a hit in the UK in 1958, until everyone discovered the B-side and it was 'flipped' – what was it?
8. In 1963 Brian Poole and the Tremeloes, and the Beatles, recorded the best-remembered versions of which standard, which had been a hit the previous year for the Isley Brothers?
9. Which Everly Brothers' oldie was recorded in concert by Simon & Garfunkel and appeared on their album 'Bridge Over Troubled Water'?
10. Little Richard had his only top three UK hit in 1956 – what was it?
11. Chuck Berry's *Come On* was covered by which British group to give them their first Top 30 hit in summer 1963?

12. Fats Domino co-wrote which song that in 1955 was a US hit for him and also, though less successfully, for Pat Boone?
13. *Lawdy Miss Clawdy* was the first recording, in 1952, by whom?
14. Which rock'n'roll performer was sometime nicknamed 'the Killer'?
15. What was the name of Buddy Holly's group?
16. The Sex Pistols had hits in 1979 with two songs originally written and recorded by whom?
17. Who was the first American rock'n'roll singer to have a US hit with a cover version of a Beatles' song, when he took *From Me To You* into the Top 100 in 1963?
18. John Preston Courville had a No. 1 on both sides of the Atlantic in 1960 with *Running Bear,* under what name?
19. Gary U.S. Bonds had a couple of hits in 1961 and then made a comeback twenty years later with *This Little Girl*, written specially for him by whom?
20. Which song was a US No. 1 in 1962 for Gene Chandler and a UK Top 10 hit in 1979 for Darts?

Answers

1. Danny Rapp
2. *You're Sixteen*
3. Buddy Knox
4. *Why Do Fools Fall in Love*
5. Bill Haley and the Comets
6. Johnny Kidd
7. *Move It*, Cliff Richard
8. *Twist and Shout*
9. *Bye Bye Love*
10. *Long Tall Sally*

11. The Rolling Stones
12. *Ain't That a Shame*
13. Lloyd Price
14. Jerry Lee Lewis
15. The Crickets
16. Eddie Cochran
17. Del Shannon
18. Johnny Preston
19. Bruce Springsteen
20. *Duke of Earl*

Tamla Motown

1. In which year did Berry Gordy Jr found Tamla Records, as the company was initially known?
2. In 1972, Motown moved its headquarters from Detroit to which other city?
3. *My Guy* was the first Motown single to reach the UK Top 10, in summer 1964, for which performer?
4. Released in 1960, which was Motown's first million-selling single in the US?
5. Which group included in its line-up at various times Eddie Kendricks, David Ruiffin, and Paul Williams?
6. Whose greatest hits on the label included *S.O.S. (Stop Her on Sight), Twenty-Five Miles*, and *War*?
7. Which was the Supremes' first US No. 1, and also their first UK hit, reaching No. 2?
8. Before launching a separate Tamla Motown label in the UK, on which label did EMI release the material?
9. Which Four Tops single was their first UK Top 40 hit, reaching No. 23 in 1965 (and No. 10 on re-release five years later)?
10. *Mercy, Mercy Me (The Ecology)* and *Inner City Blues* were singles from the groundbreaking album 'What's Going On' by whom?
11. Which instrument was played by Junior Walker of Junior Walker and the All-Stars?
12. Whose biggest UK hit, Top 10 in 1980, was *Behind the Groove*?
13. Which songwriting and production trio, responsible for many of the early successes, left

the company in 1967 over a dispute regarding profit-sharing and royalties?
14. Which transatlantic Top 10 hit included the lines, 'Evolution, revolution, gun control and sound of soul, shooting rockets to the moon, kids growing up too soon'?
15. Excluding a re-release in 1974 of *Baby Love*, which was The Supremes' last Top 40 hit in the UK?
16. Which singer and songwriter was Vice-President of the company from the mid-1960s until 1988?
17. Which Isley Brothers single reached No. 5 in the UK in 1969 but was never a hit in the US?
18. The Four Tops lasted over forty years without a change in personnel until the death from cancer in 1997 of which member?
19. Which company acquired Motown in 1999?
20. Kennedy Gordy, son of Berry Gordy Jr, had a Top 10 hit in 1984 with *Somebody's Watching Me*, under what name?

Answers

1. 1959
2. Los Angeles
3. Mary Wells
4. *Shop Around*, The Miracles
5. The Temptations
6. Edwin Starr
7. *Where Did Our Love Go*
8. Stateside
9. *I Can't Help Myself*
10. Marvin Gaye
11. Saxophone
12. Teena Marie

13. Brian Holland, Lamont Dozier, and Eddie Holland
14. *Ball of Confusion*, The Temptations
15. *Bad Weather*
16. William (Smokey) Robinson
17. *Behind A Painted Smile*
18. Laurence Payton
19. Universal Music Group
20. Rockwell

Progressive Rock

When rock met the classics.

1. Carl Palmer, the drummer with Emerson, Lake and Palmer, had previously been a member of which chart-topping outfit?
2. The Moody Blues were provided with the facilities of using an orchestra in 1967 because Deram Records wanted to release a new album showcasing their new advanced production technology. What was the resulting album?
3. Which member of Deep Purple composed their *Concerto for Group and Orchestra*?
4. 'Air Conditioning', which was the first album to be released in the UK as a picture disc as well as on black vinyl, was the debut album in 1970 for which group?
5. Alex Lifeson and Geddy Lee are members of which Canadian group?
6. The 17-minute epic *In Held Twas In I*, appears on 'Shine on Brightly', an album by which group?
7. Which Yes album is based on a concept reflecting Jon Anderson's vision of four classes of Hindu scripture, collectively named the shastras?
8. Which group was formed in 1968 by Robert Fripp?
9. At which university did the members of Van Der Graaf Generator originally meet in 1967?
10. Members from Simon Dupree and the Big Sound went on to form which 1970s group?

11. Which No 1 album from 1969 was released in a gatefold sleeve designed to open like a child's pop-up book?
12. Which UK trio released 'Black Moon', their first album for fourteen years, in 1992?
13. At one point during the height of their success in 1973, Focus had two singles simultaneously in the UK Top 20. One was *Sylvia*, which was the other?
14. Pink Floyd topped the bill at a free open air concert in June 1968 just after the release of 'A Saucerful of Secrets' at which venue?
15. Which group had minor success in the album charts in the mid-1980s with their first two albums, 'The Sentinel' and 'The Wedge'?
16. Which artist, well-known for his designs featuring fantasy landscapes, is also famous as a designer of album and CD cover art, including records by Yes, Asia, Uriah Heep and Atomic Rooster?
17. Which group, who had their greatest success between 1970 and their disbanding in 1973, released their first, unsuccessful, double A-side single *Scene Through The Eye Of A Lens/Gypsy Woman* in 1967?
18 Which single did Hawkwind withdraw from sale shortly after it entered the Top 40 in 1973, fearing accusations of opportunism, as it coincided with an IRA bombing campaign in London?
19. Which Kansas album, released in 1976, included their only UK minor hit *Carry On Wayward Son*?
20. Which was the first Western rock band to play an open-air concert in East Berlin, on 14 July 1987?

Answers

1. The Crazy World of Arthur Brown
2. 'Days of Future Passed'
3. Jon Lord
4. Curved Air
5. Rush
6. Procol Harum
7. 'Tales From Topographic Oceans'
8. King Crimson
9. Manchester
10. Gentle Giant
11. 'Stand Up'
12. Emerson, Lake and Palmer
13. *Hocus Pocus*
14. Hyde Park
15. Pallas
16. Roger Dean
17. Family
18. *Urban Guerrilla*
19. 'Leftoverture'
20. Barclay James Harvest

Glam Rock

All that glitters – or did in the 1970s.

1. Which group was previously known as Wainwright's Gentlemen?
2. Which was the only single by Gary Glitter to enter the British chart at No. 1?
3. Chas Chandler, Slade's manager, was formerly the bassist with which famous 1960s group?
4. What was the title of the first album by Wizzard?
5. Which independent record label issued the first four T. Rex singles (in other words, after they had shortened their name from Tyrannosaurus Rex)?
6. Suzi Quatro's first hit was *Can the Can*, but her previous single on the same label, Rak, was a flop – what was it?
7. Who was the lead guitarist in Geordie?
8. Which Chicory Tip hit featured a girl's name in the title?
9. Which was Alvin Stardust's second single and only No. 1?
10. What was the first Top 10 hit by Cockney Rebel?
11. 'There's a new sensation, a fabulous creation, a danceable solution to teenage revolution' are the opening lines to which Roxy Music album track?
12. Who had Top 10 hits with *The Bump, Fancy Pants,* and *Julie Anne*?
13. Who was vocalist with the New York Dolls?

14. Which was the last T. Rex single to make the UK Top 10?
15. Whose only Top 10 hit was in 1972 with *Standing In the Road*?
16. Who played oboe and saxophone with Roxy Music and also guested on Mott The Hoople's *Honaloochie Boogie* and *All the Way From Memphis*?
17. Gerry Shephard and John Springate fronted which group?
18. *Tell Him,* Hello's first Top 10 hit, had already been a success in the early 1960s for which other group?
19. *See My Baby Jive* was Wizzard's first No. 1; what was the second?
20. The Rubettes, the Glitter Band and Mud featured in which mid-1970s film?

Answers

1. Sweet
2. *I Love You Love Me Love*
3. The Animals
4. 'Wizzard Brew'
5. Fly
6. *Rolling Stone*
7. Vic Malcolm
8. *Good Grief Christina*
9. *Jealous Mind*
10. *Judy Teen*
11. *Do the Strand*
12. Kenny
13. David Johansen
14. *The Groover*
15. Blackfoot Sue
16. Andy Mackay

17. The Glitter Band
18. The Exciters
19. *Angel Fingers*
20. *Never too Young to Rock*

Punk rock

A few questions from year zero, or thenabouts.

1. After the Sex Pistols were 'sent packing' by EMI, which label did they sign with outside Buckingham Palace?
2. *New Rose* is reckoned to be the first widely released punk single, but by whom?
3. At which London venue did the Ramones, the Flamin' Groovies and the Stranglers play on 4 July 1976?
4. Which group was fronted by Poly Styrene?
5. Which Australian band had a Top 40 hit with *This Perfect Day*?
6. On which label did the Buzzcocks release *Spiral Scratch* EP in January 1977?
7. Who was the vocalist and guitarist in Stiff Little Fingers?
8. What was the Adverts' only Top 20 single?
9. In which town were the Jam formed?
10. Who played bass with the Clash?
11. *If The Kids Are United* was Sham 69's first Top 10 hit; which was the only other?
12. Whose first album was 'Pink Flag'?
13. Who was the bass guitarist with Generation X?
14. What was the Ruts' most successful UK single?
15. In which town were the Angelic Upstarts formed?
16. Who was successively drummer with London, the Damned, and later Culture Club?

17. Greg Ginn formed and led which hardcore punk band formed in California in 1976?
18. Who was the vocalist with Eddie and the Hot Rods?
19. What was the Dickies' only UK Top 10 hit?
20. Who released the EP *Love and a Molotov Cocktail* and the album *Waikiki Beach Refugees*, and also featured Hazel O'Connor's brother Neil on guitar and keyboards?

Answers

1. A&M
2. The Damned
3. The Roundhouse
4. X-Ray Spex
5. The Saints
6. New Hormones
7. Jake Burns
8. *Gary Gilmore's Eyes*
9. Woking
10. Paul Simonon
11. *Hersham Boys*
12. Wire
13. Tony James
14. *Babylon's Burning*
15. South Shields
16. Jon Moss
17. Black Flag
18. Barrie Masters
19. *Banana Splits*
20. *The Flys*

Britpop

The big sensation, albeit briefly, of the mid-1990s.

1. Who released the albums 'Smart', 'The It Girl', and 'Pleased To Meet You'?
2. When BBC Radio 6 listeners voted for their Top 40 Britpop anthems in April 2004, which one topped the poll?
3. Who was the lead singer of James until he left in 2001?
4. Which Supergrass album featured the single *St Petersburg*?
5. For which group did Noel Gallagher work as a roadie and technician prior to joining his brother Liam's group?
6. According to journalist John Harris, 'If Britpop started anywhere, it was the deluge of acclaim that greeted the first records' of which group, 'all of them audacious, successful and very, very British'?
7. Which Ocean Colour Scene album contained the Top 10 singles *The Riverboat Song*, *The Day We Caught the Train*, and *You've Got It Bad*?
8. Which group included Gary Stringer on vocals, and Kenwyn House on guitar?
9. Lush formed in 1987, but under a different name – which?
10. During what was dubbed by *NME* as the 'British Heavyweight Championship' between new singles by Blur and Oasis released simultaneously in August 1995, which Blur

single outsold Oasis' *Roll With It* to enter the singles chart at No. 1?

11. Todd Parmenter, Matt Everitt and Darren Tudgay were successively drummers with which group?

12. Guitarist and vocalist John Power left the La's in 1991 to form which group?

13. To which independent label did Oasis sign in 1993?

14. At the BRIT Awards in 1996, Jarvis Cocker of Pulp invaded the stage as a spontaneous protest during the appearance of which singer?

15. Which single by Suede, which reached No. 3 in 1994, was the last to feature guitarist Bernard Butler?

16. On which label did all Blur releases appear until 2000 when it was absorbed by EMI into Parlophone?

17. Who wrote and directed the 2003 documentary film *Live Forever: The Rise and Fall of Britpop*?

18. Where did Oasis play a two-night set in August 1996, hailed by one journalist as 'the best-ever Britpop performance'?

19. Justin Frischmann, who had a relationship with Damon Albarn of Blur, was vocalist and guitarist with Suede and then which other group?

20. Released on the label Backbeat, what was the first single by Supergrass?

Answers

1. Sleeper
2. *Common People*, Pulp
3. Tim Booth

4. 'Road To Rouen'
5. Inspiral Carpets
6. Suede
7. 'Moseley Shoals'
8. Reef
9. Baby Machines
10. *Country House*
11. Menswear
12. Cast
13. Creation
14. Michael Jackson
15. *Stay Together*
16. Food
17. John Dower
18. Knebworth
19. Elastica
20. *Caught By The Fuzz*

True Or False?

Ten of these statements are true, ten are made up. Do you know, or can you guess, which are genuine and which are the porkies?

1. Wendy Richard and Trevor Bannister had a hit single in 1975 with *Are You Being Served.*
2. When Cream disbanded in 1968, Jack Bruce was initially invited to join Led Zeppelin on bass, the arrangement being that John Paul Jones would play keyboards in what would be a five-piece group.
3. Jim Kerr and Charlie Burchill of Simple Minds were previously in a punk band called Johnny and the Self Abusers.
4. Elvis Presley was scheduled to appear on stage at the Woodstock Festival in 1969 as part of a strategy to try and bring him a more hip following, but his manager 'Colonel' Parker vetoed the idea at the last moment.
5. DJs and presenters were not allowed to announce the full title of the Sex Pistols' album 'Never Mind The Bollocks, Here's The Sex Pistols' on Radio 1 at the time of release and for some weeks thereafter, as it was deemed potentially offensive to some listeners, but they could call it 'Never Mind'.
6. In the Walker Brothers, only one of the trio was actually called Walker.
7. In 1970, Bill Oddie recorded as a single *On Ilkley Moor Bah Tat* in the style of *With A Little Help From My Friends* by Joe Cocker.
8. Norah Jones is the niece of Ravi Shankar.

9. Ken Livingstone contributed the spoken part on Blur's *Parkife.*
10. Lady Gaga said that her song *Poker Face* was about her bisexuality.
11. None of Big Country, the group led by Stuart Adamson, were born in Scotland.
12. Neil Diamond said he wrote *Sweet Caroline* for Caroline Kennedy, after seeing a picture on her on the cover of *Life*, in an equestrian riding outfit.
13. Paul McCartney played piano and sang backing vocals on the Rolling Stones' *Let's Spend The Night Together*, but was not credited at the time for contractual reasons.
14. The four members of Led Zeppelin's first recordings together were as the backing group on an album by P.J. Proby.
15. Simon Cowell formerly played drums in Take That's touring band.
16. On Status Quo's *In the Army Now*, the line 'Stand up and fight!' was shouted by John Cleese.
17. Because of the popularity of The Supremes in 1964, Brian Epstein planned to record an album the following year featuring Sandie Shaw, Dusty Springfield and Cilla Black singing together as an all-girl group.
18. Although *Smoke on the Water* is probably their best-remembered track, Deep Purple never intended to release it as a single in the UK – only as an album track.
19. Val Doonican was one of the Pogues' earliest champions in the media, and he sang chorus vocals as well as playing acoustic guitar on several of their sessions, including those for *A Fairytale of New York*.

20. Only four different albums topped the UK chart throughout 1966 – The Beatles' 'Rubber Soul' and 'Revolver', The Rolling Stones' 'Aftermath', and *The Sound of Music* original soundtrack.

Answers

1. False
2. True
3. True
4. False
5. True (the 'ban' was later rescinded)
6. False (none were)
7. True
8. False (she is his daughter)
9. False
10. True
11. True
12. True
13. False
14. True
15. False
16. False (it was by Noddy Holder)
17. False
18. True
19. False
20. True

Siblings

Which groups featured these brothers or sisters?

1. Ray and Dave Davies
2. Noel and Liam Gallagher
3. Ann and Nancy Wilson
4. Mark and David Knopfler
5. Brian, Carl and Dennis Wilson
6. John and Tom Fogerty
7. David Sylvian and Steve Jansen (their real surname was Batt)
8. Jonny and Colin Greenwood
9. Angus and Malcolm Young
10. Alex and Laddie Burke, plus Earl and Timmy Smith
11. Ron and Russell Mael
12. Ruth, June, Bonnie and Anita (whose name is part of the group name)
13. Matt and Luke Goss
14. Dave and Ron Asheton
15. Vicki and Debbi Peterson
16. Paul and Phil Hartnoll
17. Caleb, Nathan and Jared Followill
18. Win and Will Butler
19. James and Ben Johnston
20. Charlie and Craig Reid

Answers

1. The Kinks
2. Oasis
3. Heart

4. Dire Straits
5. The Beach Boys
6. Creedence Clearwater Revival
7. Japan
8. Radiohead
9. AC/DC
10. The Showstoppers
11. Sparks
12. The Pointer Sisters
13.Bros
14. Iggy and the Stooges
15. The Bangles
16. Orbital
17. Kings of Leon
18. Arcade Fire
19. Biffy Clyro
20. The Proclaimers

Lyrics

In chronological order, all these songs reached No. 1 in Britain, but which was the song? OK, have a bonus point for the artist (there are two different names for the first), and another for the year in which it got there (again, two years for the ninth...all right, that makes two more bonus points – you should be so lucky – and there goes another clue somewhere...)

1. 'I never felt more like running away, but where would I go 'cos I couldn't stay without you'
2. 'When you walk through a storm, hold your head up high'
3. 'I used to think I was livin', Baby, I was wrong, No I never knew a thing about livin', 'Til you came along'
4. 'Love was out to get me, That's the way it seemed, Disappointment haunted all my dreams'
5. 'Mr Frears had sticky-out ears, and it made him awful shy'
6. 'I dreamt that she was Lady Chatterley, and I was the gamekeeper, I dreamt that I was Da Vinci, and she was the Mona Lisa'
7. 'Well we got no class, And we got no principals, And we got no innocence, We can't even think of a word that rhymes'
8. 'That tenor horn is turning me on, he drops down to his knees'
9. 'Mama, just killed a man, put a gun against his head, pulled my trigger, now he's dead'

10. 'The silicon chip inside her head gets switched to overload'
11. 'I was sick and tired of everything, when I called you last night from Glasgow'
12. 'Tonight the music seems so loud, I wish that we could lose this crowd, Maybe it's better this way, We'd hurt each other with the things we want to say'
13. 'Now this mountain I must climb, Feels like a world upon my shoulders, And through the clouds I see love shine, It keeps me warm as life grows colder'
14. 'I need a man who'll take a chance, on a love that burns hot enough to last, So when the night falls, my lonely heart calls'
15. 'In my imagination, there is no hesitation, We walk together hand in hand, I'm dreaming'
16. 'I can't wear this uniform without some compromises, Because you'll find out that we come in different shapes and sizes'
17. 'Some days I pray for silence, and some days I pray for soul, some days I just pray to the God of Sex and Drums and Rock 'n'Roll'
18. 'So Sally can wait, she knows it's too late as she's walking on by'
19. 'Tell me you love me when you leave, You're more than a shadow, that's what I believe, You take me to places I never dreamed I'd see, Minute by minute you are the world to me'
20. 'I'll write a symphony just for you and me, If you let me love you, I'll paint a masterpiece, Just for you to see'

Answers

1. *Singing the Blues*, Guy Mitchell or Tommy Steele, both 1957
2. *You'll Never Walk Alone*, Gerry and the Pacemakers, 1963 (or The Crowd, 1985)
3. *I'm Alive*, The Hollies, 1965
4. *I'm a Believer*, The Monkees, 1967
5. *Lily the Pink*, The Scaffold, 1968
6. *Baby Jump*, Mungo Jerry, 1971
7. *School's Out*, Alice Cooper, 1972
8. *See My Baby Jive*, Wizzard, 1973
9. *Bohemian Rhapsody*, Queen, 1975 and 1991
10. *I Don't Like Mondays*, Boomtown Rats, 1979
11. *Super Trouper*, ABBA, 1980
12. *Careless Whisper*, George Michael, 1984
13. *I Want to Know What Love Is*, Foreigner, 1985
14. *I Wanna Dance With Somebody*, Whitney Houston, 1987
15. *I Should Be So Lucky*, Kylie Minogue, 1988
16. *The One and Only*, Chesney Hawkes, 1991
17. *I'd Do Anything For Love (But I Won't Do That)*, Meat Loaf, 1993
18. *Don't Look Back In Anger*, Oasis, 1996
19. *Perfect Moment*, Martine McCutcheon, 1999
20. *Are You Ready For Love*, Elton John, 2003

Duets

The following songs were major hits, in most cases topping the charts on one if not both sides of the Atlantic. (Admittedly, calling one of them a song involves a little artistic licence, maybe). But who were the artists?

1. *You're The One That I Want*, 1978
2. *Easy Lover*, 1985
3. *Somethin' Stupid*, 1967
4. *No More Tears (Enough Is Enough)*, 1979
5. *Ebony And Ivory*, 1982
6. *My Boo*, 2004
7. *I Knew You Were Waiting For Me*, 1987
8. *When You Believe*, 1998
9. *Up Where We Belong*, 1982
10. *I'm Your Angel*, 1998
11. *Je T'Aime...Moi Non Plus*, 1969
12. *I Just Can't Stop Loving You*, 1987
13. *We've Got Tonight*, 1983
14. *Where The Wild Roses Grow*, 1995
15. *I'll Be Missing You*, 1997
16. *It's My Party*, 1981
17. *Never Be The Same Again*, 2000
18. *I Know Him So Well*, 1985
19. *What a Wonderful World*, 2007
20. *I'm Real*, 2001

Answers

1. John Travolta and Olivia Newton-John
2. Philip Bailey and Phil Collins

3. Frank and Nancy Sinatra
4. Barbra Streisand and Donna Summer
5. Paul McCartney and Stevie Wonder
6. Usher and Alicia Keys
7. Aretha Franklin and George Michael
8. Mariah Carey and Whitney Houston
9. Joe Cocker and Jennifer Warnes
10. R. Kelly and Celine Dion
11. Jane Birkin and Serge Gainsbourg
12. Michael Jackson and Siedah Garrett
13. Kenny Rogers and Sheena Easton
14, Kylie Minogue and Nick Cave
15. Puff Daddy and Faith Evans
16. Dave Stewart and Barbara Gaskin
17. Melanie C and Left Eye Lopes
18. Elaine Paige and Barbara Dickson
19. Eva Cassidy and Katie Melua
20. J. Lo and Ja Rule

Multiple Choice

Which is the correct answer out of the following?

1. Barry, Robin and Maurice Gibb of the Bee Gees were born where - (a) Isle of Man, (b) Australia, (c) Manchester, (d) London
2. The Humblebums were for the most part a duo featuring Gerry Rafferty and which stand-up comedian – (a) Jack Dee, (b) Eddie Izzard, (c) Billy Connolly, (d) Ben Elton
3. The Dixieland Jazz Band recorded the first ever jazz band single, but in which year - (a) 1917, (b) 1920, (c) 1923, (d) 1926
4. When the first Glastonbury Festival was held in 1970, what was the admission price - (a) Free, (b) 10/-, (c) £1, (d) £2
5. In which year was *Melody Maker* first published - (a) 1921, (b) 1926, (c) 1938, (d) 1949
6. On which island was Rihanna born - (a) Isle of Man, (b) Isle of Wight, (c) Jamaica, (d) Barbados
7. In August 1970 Emerson, Lake & Palmer played their first-ever gig at a venue in which city - (a) Southampton, (b) Plymouth, (c) Birmingham, (d) Newcastle
8. In 1974, Brian May of Queen was invited to join which band - (a) The Rolling Stones, (b) The Faces, (c) Led Zeppelin, (d) Sparks
9. In which westcountry seaside town was *The Pirates of Penzance* first performed in public, in 1879 - (a) Plymouth, (b) Paignton, (c) Padstow, (d) Penzance

10. Which was the only member of ABBA who could read music – (a) Bjorn, (b) Benny, (c) Agnetha, (d) Frida
11. When Freddie Mercury was introduced to Sid Vicious, he allegedly greeted him as – (a) Mr Ferocious, (b) Mr Ferret, (c) Slippery Sid, (d) Daffodil
12. Richard Branson was originally going to name his company one of these, until it became Virgin Records – (a) The Mighty Groove, (b) Ultimate, (c) Flash in the Pan, (d) Slipped Disc
13. Davy Jones of the Monkees appeared in one episode of which TV soap opera – (a) *Crossroads*, (b) *Coronation Street*, (c) *Eldorado*, (d) *East Enders*
14. In 1969, Fleetwood Mac almost signed with which record label – (a) Apple, (b) Virgin, (c) Harvest, (d) Vertigo
15. T. Rex's *Ride a White Swan* included which rock'n'roll track as one of the cuts on the B-side – (a) *Great Balls of Fire*, (b) *Johnny B. Goode*, (c) *At The Hop*, (d) *Summertime Blues*
16. In 1963 The Rolling Stones recorded a TV commercial advertising what – (a) Washing powder, (b) Rice Krispies, (c) Extra strong mints, (d) Coca-cola
17. The lyrics of The Jam's song *Time for Truth* made a reference to Uncle Jimmy, but who did they mean – (a) James Dean, (b) James Brown, (c) James Callaghan, (d) Paul Weller's uncle
18. Kyle Minogue is said to be an avid player of which game – (a) Chess, (b) Scrabble, (c) Monopoly, (d) Halma
19. In the BBC's adaptation of John Gay's *The Beggar's Opera* in 1982, who starred as Macheath – (a) Ringo Starr, (b) Steve Winwood, (c) Roger Daltrey, (d) Sting

20. In 1980, who published the novel *The Great Trouser Mystery* – (a) Bill Wyman, (b) Steve Winwood, (c) Phil Lynott, (d) Graham Parker

Answers

1. (a) Isle of Man
2. (c) Billy Connolly
3. (a) 1917
4. (c) £1
5. (b) 1926
6. (d) Barbados
7. (b) Plymouth
8. (d) Sparks
9. (b) Paignton
10. (c) Agnetha
11. (a) Mr Ferocious
12. (d) Slipped Disc
13. (b) *Coronation Street*
14. (a) Apple
15. (d) *Summertime Blues*
16. (b) Rice Krispies
17. (c) James Callaghan
18. (b) Scrabble
19. (c) Roger Daltrey
20. (d) Graham Parker

The Beatles – as a group

1. What was the original working title of the film *Help*!
2. Two Beatles singles held the No. 1 position in the UK for seven weeks. *From Me To You* was the first – which was the second?
3. What was John Lennon wearing in the photograph on the front cover of *Abbey Road*?
4. Klaus Voorman designed the sleeve of *Revolver*. With which group was he bass guitarist at the time?
5. Which song did the Beatles sing with Morecambe & Wise on an episode of their show recorded in 1963? (Wise sang with them, Morecambe heckled)
6. When the group played the Royal Variety Performance in 1963, John Lennon asked those in the cheap seats to clap their hands, and what did he tell the rest to do?
7. The Beatles' last hit of the 1960s was *Something*, a double A-side with which other track?
8. Which rock'n'roll song, not written by the group, appeared as the only track never before released in the UK on the 1966 album *A Collection Of Beatles Oldies*? (It had been on the US album 'Beatles VI' in 1965)
9. The Beatles launched their own record label in 1968 named after their boutique - what was the name?

10. Which was the first George Harrison song to become a Top 20 hit in Britain by another artiste or group?

Answers

1. *Eight Arms To Hold You*
2. *Hello Goodbye*
3. A white suit
4. Manfred Mann
5. *Moonlight Bay*
6. Rattle their jewellery
7. *Come Together*
8. *Bad Boy*
9. Apple
10. *If I Needed Someone*, by the Hollies

Beatles' cover versions

Which artists had the most successful (in other words, the highest-charting in the UK) versions of the following Lennon-McCartney compositions, in some cases written specially for them?

1. *Step Inside Love*
2. *A World Without Love*
3. *Girl*
4. *Got To Get You Into My Life*
5. *I Wanna Be Your Man*
6. *Ob La Di, Ob La Da*
7. *Bad To Me*
8. *The Long And Winding Road*
9. *Here, There and Everywhere*
10. *Dear Prudence*

Answers

1. Cilla Black
2. Peter and Gordon
3. St Louis Union
4. Cliff Bennett and the Rebel Rousers
5. The Rolling Stones
6. Marmalade
7. Billy J. Kramer and the Dakotas
8. Will Young and Gareth Gates
9. Emmylou Harris
10. Siouxsie and the Banshees

John Lennon

1. Which song on the 'Imagine' album was largely a thinly-veiled attack on Paul McCartney's music?
2. Which David Bowie hit, a US No. 1 and UK Top 20 hit in 1975, was co-written by and features Lennon?
3. Which album did Lennon produce for Nilsson in 1974?
4. *Imagine* was first released as a single in Britain in 1975, largely to promote which compilation album of his post-Beatles work?
5. Which was the first single to be released from 'Double Fantasy', and was in the charts at the time he was murdered?
6. Which choir can be heard on *Happy Xmas War Is Over*?
7. When *Imagine* was released as a single in the UK, what was on the B-side?
8. Which American group backed him on the album 'Sometime In New York City'?
9. Lennon married Yoko Ono in 1969 in the British Consulate Office, but where?
10. Which Chuck Berry song was he accused of plagiarizing for *Come Together*, which resulted in an out-of-court settlement in 1976?

Answers

1. *How Do You Sleep*
2. *Fame*
3. 'Pussy Cats'

4. 'Shaved Fish'
5. *(Just Like) Starting Over*
6. Harlem Community Choir
7. *Working Class Hero*
8. Elephants Memory
9. Gibraltar
10. *You Can't Catch Me*

Paul McCartney

1. Which Liberal Member of Parliament was among the famous faces shown on the sleeve of 'Band On The Run'?
2. *Mull of Kintyre* by Wings was officially released as a double A-side with which other track?
3. What was the title of the 1984 hit credited to Paul McCartney and the Frog Chorus?
4. With whom did McCartney co-write five of the songs on 'Flowers In The Dirt'?
5. The Fireman is a duo comprising McCartney and who else?
6. Which classical oratorio composed by him was recorded by the London Symphony Orchestra and released in 1997?
7. The live version of *Coming Up*, which was a US No. 1 in 1980, was recorded the previous year at which venue?
8. For which act did he produce *Liverpool Lou*, a Top 10 UK hit in 1974?
9. Under what group name did he and other musicians including Paul Weller and Noel Gallagher record *Come Together* in 1995 on 'Help!', the War Child benefit album?
10. What was the title of the Wings triple live album released in 1977?

Answers

1. Clement Freud
2. *Girls School*

3. *We All Stand Together*
4. Elvis Costello
5. Youth (Martin Glover)
6. 'Standing Stone'
7. Glasgow Apollo
8. The Scaffold
9. The Smokin' Mojo Filters
10. 'Wings Over America'

George Harrison

1. Which song by Harrison made him the first and last former Beatle to have a solo UK No. 1?
2. On which Top 10 hit by Belinda Carlisle did he play lead guitar?
3. By what name was he credited when he played guitar on one track of Cream's final album 'Goodbye'?
4. What was his record label, which he named after his 1974 solo album?
5. Who wrote his 1987 hit *Got My Mind Set On You*?
6. On whose all-star album did he collaborate with on *Horse To the Water* in 2001?
7. On behalf of which political organisation did he play a benefit concert at the Royal Albert Hall in 1992?
8. Which Cole Porter song did he cover on the album 'Thirty-Three And A Third'?
9. On the first Traveling Wilburys album in 1988, which alias did he assume?
10. To which charity did profits go from the Concert for George, staged on the first anniversary of his death?

Answers

1. *My Sweet Lord*
2. *Leave a Light On*
3. L'Angelo Misterioso
4. Dark Horse
5. Rudy Clark

6. Jools Holland
7. Natural Law Party
8. *True Love*
9. Nelson Wilbury
10. Material World Charitable Foundation

Ringo Starr

1. *If You've Got Trouble*, featuring Starr on vocals, was not released at the time and first appeared on 'Anthology 2'. For which album by the group had it been originally intended?
2. What was his first solo hit in 1971 and also the song which he performed at the Concert For Bangla Desh later that year?
3. *Photograph*, a No. 1 US and top ten UK hit in 1973, had originally been written with which female vocalist in mind?
4. Which track on The Beatles' 'White Album' did he write as well as sing?
5. What was the title of his minor Top 75 hit in 1992?
6. Which song did John Lennon contribute to the album 'Ringo' in 1973?
7. In 1985, Starr was part of a group with George Harrison, Eric Clapton, Dave Edmunds and others who recorded a TV special at Limehouse Studios backing which veteran rock'n'roll performer?
8. With which Platters hit did he have a Top 30 UK hit in 1974?
9. For which children's TV series, first made and shown in 1984, did he provide the narration?
10. In 1970 he released two solo albums, the first being 'Sentimental Journey', which made the UK Top 10. Which was the second, which failed to chart?

Answers

1. 'Help!'
2. *It Don't Come Easy*
3. Cilla Black
4. *Don't Pass Me By*
5. *The Weight Of the World*
6. *I'm The Greatest*
7. Carl Perkins
8. *Only You*
9. *Thomas the Tank Engine*
10. 'Beaucoups of Blues'

Sir George Martin

1. Which institution did Martin attend from 1947 to 1950, studying piano and oboe?
2. When he joined EMI Records in 1950, he was initially assistant to the then head of Parlophone Records – what was his name?
3. Which album did he produce in 1957, featuring the Goons, Peter Cook and other contemporary humorists, the title of which was a spoof on a recent World War II movie?
4. Which song by Mitch Murray did Martin persuade the Beatles to record at their first session with him for EMI on 4 September, although they refused to release it as a single? (It later became a No. 1 for Gerry and the Pacemakers).
5. Who was 'The man with the golden voice', the balladeer for whom Martin produced several UK hits in the first half of the sixties?
6. *Anyone Who Had a Heart* was the first of two consecutive UK No. 1 hits for Cilla Black, produced by Martin in 1964; which was the second?
7. On which Beatles song, a track from 'Rubber Soul', did Martin play a Bach-inspired baroque piano passage which he had written himself (although he received no joint composing credit)?
8. Which James Bond movie song, recorded by Wings and a hit in 1973, was produced and arranged by Martin?
9. Which American group released the 1980 album 'All Shook Up', a Martin production?
10. Martin also produced Ultravox's 1982 album 'Quartet'; which was the first of four singles taken

from the album, and the only one to reach the UK Top 10?

Answers

1. London Guildhall School of Music and Drama
2. Oscar Preuss
3. 'Bridge on the River Wye'
4. *How Do You Do It?*
5. Matt Monro
6. *You're My World*
7. *In My Life*
8. *Live and Let Die*
9. Cheap Trick
10. *Reap the Wild Wind*

The Rolling Stones

1. At which venue did the group make their first live appearance, in July 1962?
2. Under which pseudonym did Mick Jagger and Keith Richards write some of their earlier B-sides?
3. Which was the group's first A-side to be a Jagger-Richard composition?
4. *That Girl Belongs To Yesterday* was the first Jagger-Richard song to be a UK Top 10 hit for somebody else – who?
5. 'I was drowned, I was washed up and left for dead' is a line from which song?
6. Which famous cookery writer, who was little-known at the time, prepared the cake which was photographed on the sleeve of 'Let It Bleed'?
7. With which band did Richards and Ron Wood tour the US in 1979, specially formed for the purpose?
8. Who was their long-serving roadie and regular keyboard player, who died suddenly in 1985?
9. After Bill Wyman retired, who replaced him in the group on bass guitar?
10. Which was their last single to make the Top 10 in Britain?

Answers

1. The Marquee, London
2. Nanker Phelge
3. *The Last Time*

4. Gene Pitney
5. *Jumpin' Jack Flash*
6. Delia Smith
7. The New Barbarians
8. Ian Stewart
9. Darryl Jones
10. *Start Me Up*

Frank Sinatra

1. Whose big band did Sinatra join in November 1939 after the departure of previous vocalist Jack Leonard?
2. Which TV special and album did he record in 1973, thus marking the end of his first, short-lived retirement?
3. In which New Jersey town was he born in 1915?
4. Which album, released in 1964, was a collaboration with Count Basie, and also his first recording with Quincy Jones?
5. Which member of the Four Seasons wrote the music for his 1970 album 'Watertown'?
6. Which of his songs topped the US and UK chart in 1966?
7. In the 1950s, whose music did he describe as 'a rancid smelling aphrodisiac' (although after his death he told his audience at a concert that 'we lost a good friend today')?
8. At which Los Angeles venue was the birthday tribute, '80 Years My Way', held in 1995?
9. Which bandleader backed him on his Madison Square Garden concert in October 1974, televised and later released as 'The Main Event – Live'?
10. Which was his last solo album, released in 1984 and his only one to appear on the Qwest label?

Answers

1. Tommy Dorsey
2. 'Ol' Blue-Eyes is Back'
3. Hoboken
4. 'It Might As Well Be Swing'
5. Bob Gaudio
6. *Strangers in the Night*
7. Elvis Presley
8. The Shrine Auditorium
9. Woody Herman
10. 'LA Is My Lady'

Bing Crosby

1. What was Bing Crosby's real name?
2. To which American President, who held office between 1923 and 1929, was he a seventh cousin?
3. In which film, made in 1942, did he sing *White Christmas*?
4. Which was his first single to make the UK charts, reaching No. 3 over Christmas 1952?
5. With which vocal group did he appear in *The Road to Rio*, singing *You Don't Have to Know the Language*?
6. At which British venue did he record a live album in June and July 1976, which entered the UK Top 10 a month after his death?
7. With which singer did he record the album 'A Couple of Song and Dance Men' in 1975?
8. Which single did he promote on *Top of the Pops* and *Parkinson* on BBC TV in 1975, resulting in a Top 50 hit and a Top 30 album of which it was the title track?
9. At which British venue did he make his final live appearance on 10 October 1977, four days before his death?
10. With which British singer did he record a Christmas special in September 1977, from which the duet *The Little Drummer Boy/Peace on Earth* was extracted as a No. 3 single five years later?

Answers

1. Harry Lillis Crosby Jr.
2. Calvin Coolidge

3. *Holiday Inn*
4. *The Isle of Innisfree*
5. The Andrews Sisters
6. London Palladium
7. Fred Astaire
8. *That's What Life is All About*
9. Brighton Centre
10. David Bowie

Elvis Presley

1. What was Elvis Presley's first film, made in 1956?
2. What was the name of his mansion in Memphis?
3. Who recorded the original UK hit version, in 1967, of his 1971 success *There Goes My Everything*?
4. Which of his hits had just entered the UK singles chart at the time of his death and went on to become his 17th No. 1?
5. Which fellow rock'n'roll star was arrested outside his home in November 1976, carrying a pistol, allegedly drunk and demanding to see him?
6. What was his second forename?
7. In which city did he play his final concert on 26 June 1977?
8. Which President of the United States gave him a Bureau of Narcotics and Dangerous Drugs badge?
9. Which remixed single became a British top five hit for him in 2003?
10. Who wrote *Suspicious Minds*, the single which would become his final US No. 1 in November 1969?

Answers

1. *Love Me Tender*
2. Graceland
3. Engelbert Humperdinck

4. *Way Down*
5. Jerry Lee Lewis
6. Aaron
7. Indianapolis
8. Richard Nixon
9. *Rubberneckin'*
10. Mark James

Chuck Berry

1. Which blues musician originally put him Chuck Berry in touch with Chess Records while he was playing in Chicago in 1955?
2. Although never released as a single in the UK, what was his first US hit, reaching No. 5 in the summer of 1955?
3. Which single reached No. 2 in the US in March 1958 and No. 13 in the UK two months later?
4. The documentary *Jazz On a Summer's Day* captured his live performance in July 1958 at what event?
5. Which of his songs was covered on the fourth Beatles' album, 'Beatles For Sale', with producer George Martin on piano?
6. At which British event in 1972 did he record *My Ding-a-Ling*, later released as a single and reaching No. 1 on both sides of the Atlantic?
7. Although he later returned to Chess Records, with which label did he sign in June 1966 for a $50,000 advance?
8. In which year was he sentenced to four months' prison for tax evasion in 1973?
9. Who organised a concert and put together a backing band at a concert at the St Fox Theater, St Louis, to celebrate his 60th birthday in 1986?
10. What was the title of the UK-only TV-advertised compilation LP, released in February 1977 and reaching No. 7?

Answers

1. Muddy Waters
2. *Maybelline*
3. *Sweet Little Sixteen*
4. The Newport Jazz Festival
5. *Rock'n'Roll Music*
6. Lanchester Arts Festival
7. Mercury
8. 1979
9. Keith Richards
10. 'Motorvatin"

Roy Orbison

1. Which was Orbison's only single to reach No. 1 in the UK and US?
2. With whom did he write several of his early hits including *Uptown, Only the Lonely*, and *Running Scared*?
3. To which label did he move in the US in 1965 after leaving Monument Records?
4. Which female artist had a No. 3 hit in the US in 1977 with *Blue Bayou*, something which he acknowledged gave him a higher profile after a period of little success?
5. In which film, directed by David Lynch, did Roy unsuccessfully try to resist use of his song *In Dreams*?
6. Where was the star-studded TV special *A Black and White Night* recorded in September 1987?
7. Which of his singles reached No. 27 in the UK and No. 1 in Australia in 1969?
8. Which duo recorded his song *Claudette* as the B-side of a No. 1 hit they released in 1958?
9. On which track on 'Traveling Wilburys Vol 1' did he sing lead vocal?
10. *You Got It* was co-written by him with Jeff Lynne and which other artist?

Answers

1. *Oh, Pretty Woman*
2. Joe Melson
3. MGM

4. Linda Ronstadt
5. *Blue Velvet*
6. Ambassador Hotel's Cocoanut Grove, Los Angeles
7. *Penny Arcade*
8. The Everly Brothers (the A-side being *All I Have to Do is Dream*)
9. *Not Alone Any More*
10. Tom Petty

Johnny Cash

1. Which group did Cash form in the early 1950s while serving with the US Air Force?
2. The A-side of his first single released on the Sun label in 1955 was *Hey Porter*; what was on the B-side?
3. Which Bob Dylan song became his first UK hit, reaching No. 28 in June 1965?
4. In which English city did he begin a 13-date UK tour in May 1968?
5. Which live album topped the US charts and made No. 2 in the UK in 1969, and spawned the Top 10 hit *A Boy Named Sue*?
6. Which group, formed in 1984, included Cash, Waylon Jennings, Willie Nelson and Kris Kristofferson?
7. Which single, recorded with the Evangel Temple Choir on backing vocals, became a transatlantic Top 10 hit in the summer of 1972?
8. In which year was he inducted into the Rock and Roll Hall of Fame?
9. In September 1985 Cash took part in the recording of an album, Class of '55, intended as a tribute to Elvis Presley, featuring other artists who had also originally begun their careers with Sun Records in the 1950s. Two of them were Jerry Lee Lewis and Roy Orbison; who was the other?
10. Which album, released in 1996, included appearances from Tom Petty and the Heartbreakers, plus members of Fleetwood Mac and the Red Hot Chili Peppers?

Answers

1. The Landsberg Barbarians
2. *Cry Cry Cry*
3. *It Ain't Me Babe*
4. Manchester (the venue being the Free Trade Hall)
5. 'Johnny Cash at San Quentin'
6. The Highwaymen
7. *A Thing Called Love*
8. 1992
9. Carl Perkins
10. 'Unchained', sometimes known as 'American II; Unchained'

The Everly Brothers

1. For which small US label did the Everly Brothers record from 1957 until 1960, although their UK releases during that period appeared on the London label?
2. Which husband and wife team wrote several of their early hits, including *Wake Up Little Susie*, *Bird Dog* and *All I Have To Do Is Dream*?
3. Which British group backed them on their 1966 album 'Two Yanks in England'?
4. What was the title of their first album for Warner Bros, released in May 1960, reaching No. 9 in the US and No. 2 in the UK?
5. Under which alias did Don Everly record a big band instrumental version of *Pomp and Circumstance*, arranged by Neal Hefti, which became a US Top 40 hit in 1961?
6. Which single failed to reach the US Top 100 but was a No. 2 hit in the UK in 1965, and was later covered by Status Quo and also Bryan Ferry?
7. Which song on Roy Wood's 1975 album 'Mustard' features Phil Everly on guest vocal?
8. Which self-penned single did Phil Everly release as a single in the US in 1980 and the UK the following spring, although it was never a hit?
9. What was the title of the Brothers' last recording together in 1996, a song on Andrew Lloyd Webber and Jim Steinman's *Whistle Down the Wind*?
10. Where in London did the Brothers play their reunion concert in September 1983, recorded for

a live album and broadcast on cable TV, with Pete Wingfield as musical director?

Answers

1. Cadence
2. Felice and Boudleaux Bryant
3. The Hollies
4. 'It's Everly Time'
5. Adrian Kimberly
6. *The Price of Love*
7. *Get On Down Home*
8. *Dare to Dream Again*
9. *Cold*
10. Royal Albert Hall

Cliff Richard

1. On which show did Cliff Richard make his first TV appearance in September 1958?
2. Which guitarist and former member of The Shadows produced his 1976 album 'I'm Nearly Famous'?
3. Which of his singles, becoming a Top 20 hit in 1966, had been written by Mick Jagger and Keith Richard?
4. From which movie soundtrack was *Sudddenly*, a duet with Olivia Newton-John, taken?
5. Which new release did he promote with a performance on *Top Of The Pops* in 1975, then say he would never sing again unless all the words were changed, after he was made aware of the true meaning of the song?
6. Which of his songs was the UK No. 1 at Christmas in 1990?
7. Which rock guitarist performed *Move It* with him at the Golden Jubilee Party at the Palace concert in 2002, and also on a re-recording of the song, released as a double A-side single in 2006?
8. In January 1963 Cliff Richard and the Shadows had a double A-side at No. 1. One song was *The Next Time*; what was the other?
9. Which was his 100th album, released in November 2013?
10. Which was his 100th UK single, a No. 2 hit in 1990?

Answers

1. *Oh Boy*
2. Bruce Welch
3. *Blue Turns To Grey*
4. *Xanadu*
5. *Honky Tonk Angel*
6. *Saviour's Day*
7. Brian May
8. *Bachelor Boy*
9. 'The Fabulous Rock'n'Roll Songbook'
10. *The Best Of Me*

Brian Poole and The Tremeloes

1. Brian Poole and The Tremeloes were one of two groups who auditioned for Decca Records on new year's day 1962 and were accordingly signed by the company. Which was the other group who were (famously) rejected?
2. Which was the group's first Decca single, and which failed to chart?
3. Which of their singles topped the UK chart for three weeks in October 1963, knocking The Beatles' *She Loves You* aside in the process?
4. Who recorded the original version of *Blessed*, the group's first single without Poole, released in the summer of 1966?
5. With which group did Poole release two unsuccessful singles on the President label in 1969?
6. *Silence is Golden*, The Tremeloes' No. 1 of 1967, had originally appeared as the B-side of Rag Doll, a No. 2 hit for which other group in 1964?
7. Which song by Mitch Murray and Peter Callender appeared on the first Tremeloes album in 1967 and was re-recorded to become their third Top 10 single?
8. Which guitarist replaced Rick West in the group in 1972, although West later rejoined?
9. Under what alias did the group release their 1975 album 'Don't Let the Music Die'?
10. Which Europop hit gave the group a minor hit (No. 91) in 1983, but eclipsed by the original

by F.R. David which reached No. 2 in the UK at the same time?

Answers

1. The Beatles
2. *Twist Little Sister*
3. *Do You Love Me*
4. Simon and Garfunkel
5. The Seychelles
6. The Four Seasons
7. *Even the Bad Times Are Good*
8. Bob Benham
9. Space
10. *Words*

The Hollies

1. The Hollies started as a duo formed by Allan Clarke and Graham Nash, modelled on the Everly Brothers, but under what name?
2. At which Manchester venue did the group perform their first gig as The Hollies in December 1962?
3. Which was their first UK hit, a cover of an old Coasters' song, reaching the Top 30 in the summer of 1963?
4. Which was their first single to reach the US Top Ten, a transatlantic hit in 1966?
5. Two acts covered The Hollies' *Have You Ever Loved Somebody* from the album 'Evolution' in 1967 as a single, and both just made the UK Top 50. Can you name either?
6. Which Clarke-Nash song did the group donate to the various artists album 'No One's Gonna Change Our World', released in 1969 with royalties going to the World Wildlife Fund?
7. After Clarke's departure, which was the next album the group released in October 1972, with Mikael Rickfors as vocalist?
8. Who wrote *Soldier's Song*, a UK Top 50 hit in 1980?
9. Which former member and bass guitarist with Mud joined the group in the mid-1980s?
10. Which was the only song the group recorded with Carl Wayne on vocals, the only previously unreleased track on their 2003 'Greatest Hits' compilation?

Answers

1. Ricky and Dane Young
2. The Oasis Club
3. *(Ain't That) Just Like Me*
4. Bus Stop
5. The Searchers; Paul and Barry Ryan (reaching No. 48 and No. 49 respectively)
6. *Wings*
7. 'Romany'
8. Mike Batt
9. Ray Stiles
10. *How Do I Survive*

Tom Jones

1. Tom Jones's first hit was *It's Not Unusual*, but to whom was the song originally offered?
2. Which song, a hit for him in 1967, was co-written and previously recorded without success by Lonnie Donegan?
3. From which musical was the 1987 hit *A Boy From Nowhere* taken?
4. With which group did he have a hit in 1999 with *Mama Told Me Not To Come*?
5. Which song was a minor hit for him in 1974 and went on to become a Top 10 hit for Status Quo in 1981?
6. With which male vocalist did he perform on a medley at the BRIT Awards ceremony in 1998?
7. Which album, released in 2010 and reaching No. 2 in the UK, had been the subject of a leaked e-mail prior to release from the Vice-President of Island Records to his colleagues, demanding that they 'pull this project immediately or get my money back'?
8. With which keyboard player and TV presenter did he record and release an album, named after both of them, in 2004?
9. In which year was he knighted by the Queen?
10. Which song was a minor UK hit in 1977, and had been No. 1 on the US country chart the previous year?

Answers

1. Sandie Shaw

2. *I'll' Never Fall In Love Again*
3. Matador
4. The Stereophonics
5. *Something 'Bout You Baby I Like*
6. Robbie Williams
7. 'Praise And Blame'
8. Jools Holland
9. 2006
10. *Say You'll Stay Until Tomorrow*

Dusty Springfield

1. Which of Dusty Springfield's hits was featured on the first edition of *Top Of The Pops* in January 1964?
2. In 1961, which was the first Top 20 UK hit for The Springfields?
3. Who played piano on *In The Middle Of Nowhere*?
4. Which song did she record in 1967 for the movie *Peking Medallion*?
5. *Son Of A Preacher Man* was a track from which album?
6. On which 1974 hit by Elton John was she one of the backing vocalists?
7. With which British singer did she have a minor hit in 1993 with the duet *Heart And Soul*?
8. Which of her hits in 1989 was featured in the movie *Scandal*?
9. Who produced her 1978 album 'It Begins Again'?
10. On which single in 1987 by Richard Carpenter did she sing backing vocals?

Answers

1. *I Only Want To Be With You*
2. *Bambino*
3. Alan Price
4. *The Corrupt Ones*
5. 'Dusty In Memphis'
6. The Bitch Is Back
7. Cilla Black

8. *Nothing Has Been Proved*
9. Roy Thomas Baker
10. *Something In Your Eyes*

Bob Dylan

1. What is the 11-minute closing track on 'Blonde on Blonde', taking up side four on the original vinyl issue in its entirety?
2. Who was the boxing champion Hurricane, as in the song of that name?
3. Which song, an album track from 1966, was remixed by Mark Ronson and became a minor UK hit in 2007?
4. On which album did Dylan feature three tracks from his performance at the Isle of Wight festival in 1969?
5. Which was the first album on which he was backed by musicians using electric instruments?
6. At which venue did he play a concert on 17 May 1966, later released on album, where a heckler from the audience called out 'Judas'?
7. Which female vocalist had a hit in 2008 with *Make You Feel my Love*?
8. On which song recorded by Harry Belafonte did he make his first appearance on record, playing harmonica?
9. Which of his albums included guest appearances from George Harrison, Elton John and Slash?
10. With which singer did he duet on *Girl From The North Country* on 'Nashville Skyline'?

Answers

1. *Sad-Eyed Lady Of the Lowlands*
2. Ruben Carter

3. *Most Likely You Go Your Way (And I'll Go Mine)*
4. 'Self-Portrait'
5. 'Bringing It All Back Home'
6. Manchester Free Trade Hall (although for years it was thought to be the Royal Albert Hall, London – so either answer is allowable)
7. Adele
8. *Midnight Special*
9. 'Under The Red Sky'
10. Johnny Cash

Leonard Cohen

1. Who produced and arranged 'New Skin For the Old Ceremony', and toured with Cohen in the UK, US and Canada from 1974 to 1976 to promote the album?
2. In which year did he appear at the Montreal Jazz Festival and on the Pyramid Stage at Glastonbury?
3. Who sang the backing vocals on the first album, 'Songs of Leonard Cohen'?
4. Which track on 'Songs of Love and Hate' was recorded live at the Isle of Wight Festival in 1970?
5. Who was the former manager whom he sued in 2005 for misappropriation of funds?
6. Who made the Top 50 in 1992 with a cover version of *Lover Lover Lover*?
7. Where did he spend five years in seclusion between 1994 and 1999?
8. What was the title of the live album recorded on the 1979 tour, rejected for release by Columbia in 1980 but issued with a revised track listing in 2000?
9. Which western movie, directed by Robert Altman in 1971, featured three songs from the debut album on the soundtrack?
10. Which album, released in 1987, shares a title with one of the last hits by Wham!?

Answers

1. John Lissauer

2. 2008
3. Nancy Priddy
4. *Sing Another Song, Boys*
5. Kelley Lynch
6. Ian McCulloch
7. Mount Baldy Zen Center, near Los Angeles
8. 'Field Commander Cohen'
9. *McCabe and Mrs Miller*
10. 'I'm Your Man'

Joni Mitchell

1. What was the name of Mitchell's 1969 album, featuring her original versions of *Both Sides Now* and *Chelsea Morning*?
2. Which Scottish rock group took their version of *This Flight Tonight* into the UK Top 20 in 1973?
3. Released in 1974, which was her first fully electric album?
4. From her 1982 album 'Wild Things Run Fast', which Elvis Presley song gave her a US Top 50 hit that same year?
5. What was the title of her live album, recorded at the Universal Amphitheatre, Universal City, CA, in August 1974?
6. What was the name of the Canadian exhibition of art, music and culture held at the Broadgate Centre in London in September 1990, at which she exhibited several of her paintings?
7. Which album, released in 1994, marked her return to the Reprise label after a 23-year gap?
8. Which British musician co-produced her 1985 album 'Dog Eat Dog'?
9. Which song did she sing when taking part in Roger Waters' staging of 'The Wall' at the site of the Berlin Wall in July 1990?
10. To which then recently deceased jazz musician did she release a tribute album, named after him, in 1979?

Answers

1. 'Clouds'
2. Nazareth
3. 'Court And Spark'
4. *You're So Square (Baby I Don't Care)*
5. 'Miles Of Aisles'
6. Canada in the City
7. 'Turbulent Indigo'
8. Thomas Dolby
9. *Goodbye Blue Sky*
10. Charles Mingus

Neil Young

1. What is Neil Young's second forename?
2. Which was the first album, released in 1969, credited jointly to Neil Young and Crazy Horse?
3. Which of his singles was a US No. 1 and US No. 10 in 1972?
4. Which track from 'Zuma', released in 1975, had originally been recorded the previous year for another album with Crosby, Stills and Nash under a working title *Sailboat Song*?
5. Which member of Crazy Horse was fired from the group in 1972 and died shortly afterwards from a drug overdose?
6. Which group, put together specially for the sessions, backed him on his 1983 album 'Everybody's Rockin''?
7. What was the title of the documentary and concert film made at Nashville during the summer of 2005, featuring performances of his songs from Prairie Wind, directed by Jonathan Demme?
8. The title track of the 1994 album 'Sleeps With Angels' was inspired by, and in fact a tribute, to which performer who had taken his own life a couple of years earlier?
9. In January 2010 Neil Young and Dave Matthews performed the Hank Williams song *Alone and Forsaken* at a charity telethon staged in aid of which disaster which had occurred a few weeks earlier?
10. On which song from the Elton John and Leon Russell collaboration 'The Union' in 2011 did he sing the second verse and contribute backing vocals?

Answers

1. Percival
2. 'Everybody Knows This Is Nowhere'
3. *Heart of Gold*
4. *Through My Sails*
5. Danny Whitten
6. The Shocking Pinks
7. *Neil Young: Heart of Gold*
8. Kurt Cobain
9. The Haiti earthquake – the telethon was 'Hope for Haiti now: A global benefit for earthquake relief'
10. *Gone to Shiloh*

The Beach Boys

1. Which early member was replaced in 1963 by Al Jardine?
2. Which Crystals hit did The Beach Boys revive with a slightly altered title for a UK Top 10 hit in 1967?
3. Who revived their 1968 hit *Darlin'* for a Top 20 hit of his own seven years later?
4. At which New York venue did they appear in 1971 on the same bill as Grateful Dead?
5. Which Steve Winder hit of the previous year did they cover on their 1968 album 'Wild Honey'?
6. *Kokomo*, an American No. 1 in 1988, was featured on the soundtrack of which Tom Cruise movie?
7. Which album of new material was released in 2012 to celebrate their fiftieth anniversary?
8. Which Chuck Berry song gave them a Top 40 American hit in 1976?
9. At which British venue in June 1975 did they appear at a gig on the same bill as Elton John (and reportedly went down much better than he did)?
10. With which rap act did they have a No. 2 hit in Britain in 1987 with *Wipe Out*?

Answers

1. David Marks
2. *Then I Kissed Her*
3. David Cassidy

4. Fillmore East
5. *I Was Made To Love Her*
6. *Cocktail*
7. 'That's Why God Made The Radio'
8. *Rock'n'Roll Music*
9. Wembley Stadium
10. The Fat Boys

Frankie Valli and The Four Seasons

1. What is Frankie Valli's real name?
2. Who was the group's drummer, responsible for most of the vocals on the album 'Who Loves You'?
3. What was their first album on the Mowest label in 1971?
4. Which was the 1978 movie soundtrack for which Frankie Valli sang the title song?
5. Which Gaudio-Crewe song was recorded by the group in the mid-1960s and then copied by another American group who took the song to No. 1 in the UK?
6. What connected The Tremeloes, The Bay City Rollers and The Detroit Spinners with The Four Seasons?
7. Which of their early hits was also a UK Hi-NRG dance hit in 1985 for drag artist Divine?
8. Which minor hit single came from their 1977 album 'Helicon'?
9. What was their first US No. 1 single?
10. What was the title of the album on which they collaborated with the Beach Boys, and which was released in 1984?

Answers

1. Francesco Stephen Castelluccio
2. Gerry Polci
3. 'Chameleon'

4. *Grease*
5. *The Sun Ain't Gonna Shine Any More* (the group being The Walker Brothers)
6. They all had UK No. 1 singles with cover versions of their songs (*Silence Is Golden, Bye Bye Baby, Working My Way Back To You*)
7. *Walk Like a Man*
8. *Down the Hall*
9. *Sherry*
10. 'East Meets West'

Diana Ross and The Supremes

1. Which Supremes hit of 1965 was revived successfully in 1987 by Shakin' Stevens?
2. Which album by the group became their first US No. 1 album in October 1966, displacing The Beatles' 'Revolver'?
3. Which original member of the group was asked to leave in 1967 and died in poverty nine years later?
4. Which was the final single to be credited to Diana Ross and The Supremes, although ironically in view of the title Ross was the only member of the group to sing on it?
5. On which TV show did Diana Ross and The Supremes make their last appearance together before going their separate ways?
6. Which vocalist replaced Ross in The Supremes in 1970?
7. In which movie did Ross star as Billie Holliday in 1972?
8. Which husband and wife team wrote Ross's first two solo singles, *Reach Out and Touch (Somebody's Hand)* and *Ain't No Mountain High Enough*?
9. With which other Motown group did The Supremes have a transatlantic Top 20 hit in 1971 with *River Deep Mountain High*?
10. Which song by Ross, produced by Nile Rodgers and Bernard Edwards, topped the US charts for four weeks in 1980 and reached No. 2 in the UK?

Answers

1. *Come See About Me*
2. 'Supremes A'Go-Go'
3. Florence Ballard
4. *Someday We'll Be Together*
5. *The Ed Sullivan Show*
6. Jean Terrell
7. *The Lady Sings the Blues*
8. Nickolas Ashford and Valerie Simpson
9. The Four Tops
10. *Upside Down*

The Kinks

1. Which rock'n'roll standard was covered by the group as their second single?
2. *Death Of a Clown* was Dave Davies's first solo single; what was his second, and the only other one to be a hit?
3. In which westcountry town was original bassist Peter Quaife born?
4. In 1970 they were joined by a keyboard player whom they nicknamed John the Baptist, but what was his real name?
5. What was their only UK Top 20 hit while they were signed to RCA between 1971 and 1976?
6. Which singer, who led a very successful group in the 1970s, is a cousin of Ray and Dave Davies?
7. In which year did they play their last gigs as a group (so far)?
8. Which song gave them an American Top 10 hit and British Top 20 hit in 1983?
9. Complete the title of their 1970 album, 'Lola Versus...'
10. Which former member of Argent replaced Mick Avory on drums in 1984?

Answers

1. *Long Tall Sally*
2. *Suzanah's Still Alive*
3. Tavistock
4. John Gosling
5. *Supersonic Rocket Ship*

6. Steve Harley
7. 1996
8. *Come Dancing*
9. 'Powerman And The Moneygoround, Part One'
10. Bob Henrit

The Who

1. The Who released a single as The High Numbers in 1964 and it was a minor hit when reissued in 1980; what was the title?
2. The group's first singles were released on the Brunswick label. On which label formed by Robert Stigwood in 1966 did the next few appear, prior to the formation of Track Records?
3. What was their only album to top the UK charts?
4. Which of their singles made the Top 10 in 1966 and again on reissue in 1976?
5. At which university did they record their live album in 1970?
6. *Won't Get Fooled Again*, *Squeeze Box* and *You Better You Bet* all peaked at which chart position?
7. Pete Townshend's album *Iron Man* was adapted from a story by which writer, better known as a poet?
8. Who played piano on the 1971 hit *Let's See Action*?
9. As a gesture of solidarity with the Rolling Stones when Mick Jagger and Keith Richard were jailed in 1967 on drugs charges, The Who recorded two of their songs as a single. One was *The Last Time*, but what was the other?
10. *Athena*, their last new Top 40 single, was a track taken from which album?

Answers

1. *I'm The Face*
2. Reaction
3. 'Who's Next'
4. *Substitute*
5. Leeds
6. No. 9
7. Ted Hughes
8. Nicky Hopkins
9. *Under My Thumb*
10. 'It's Hard'

The Byrds

1. Which single did The Byrds release in 1964 on Elektra as The Beefeaters?
2. In the initial line-up of the group, which member played bass guitar?
3. Which World War Two song did they record as the final track on the album 'Mr Tambourine Man'?
4. Who played trumpet on their single *So You Want To Be a Rock'n'Roll Star*?
5. On the cover of the album 'The Notorious Byrd Brothers', Dave Crosby's place in the group photo was taken by what?
6. Which Joni Mitchell song did they record on their final album, released in 1973?
7. Which album did they record in 1968 shortly after guitarist Gram Parsons joined?
8. Which member was the only one present in every Byrds line-up?
9. Which Carole King and Gerry Goffin song was a US hit for the group in 1967 and had been a UK hit the previous year for Dusty Springfield?
10. At which British festival did they perform in June 1970?

Answers

1. *Please Let Me Love You*
2. Chris Hillman
3. *We'll Meet Again*
4. High Masekela
5. A horse

6. *For Free*
7. 'Sweetheart Of The Rodeo'
8. Roger (or Jim) McGuinn
9. *Goin' Back*
10. The Bath Festival of Blues and Progressive Music, Shepton Mallet

The Moody Blues

1. Who sang vocal on the group's 1965 No. 1 single *Go Now*?
2. Who produced their first album, 'The Magnificent Moodies'?
3. Which of the group's concept albums, released in 1969, was inspired by the first landing on the moon?
4. Which of their singles peaked at No. 2 in the UK chart in 1970, held off the top by the England World Cup Football Squad?
5. After the release of 'Seventh Sojourn' in 1972, which member of the group told *Rolling Stone*: 'We've got two Christians, one Mystic, one Pedantic and one Mess, and we all get on a treat'?
6. The 1975 single *Blue Guitar*, credited to Justin Hayward and John Lodge, was actually Hayward and which other contemporary group?
7. Which song gave them a Top 10 US single in 1986?
8. Prior to joining the group in 1978, of which British group had Patrick Moraz previously been a member?
9. The US hits *The Voice* and *Gemini Dream* were taken from which album?
10. At which charity concert did they top the bill in March 1986?

Answers

1. Denny Laine
2. Denny Cordell

3. 'To Our Children's Children's Children'
4. *Question*
5. Graeme Edge
6. 10cc
7. *Your Wildest Dreams*
8. Yes
9. 'Long Distance Voyager'
10. Birmingham Heartbeat, Children's Hospital

Pink Floyd

1. What was Pink Floyd's first Top 10 single in the UK?
2. After Syd Barrett left the group in 1968, which member was primarily responsible for their lyrics?
3. At which club near Kensington High Street did they become the resident band in their early days?
4. Why was their debut single *Arnold Layne* banned by some radio stations?
5. Which event at Alexandra Palace did they headline on 29 April 1967?
6. Which member of the group produced The Damned's second album 'Music For Pleasure' in 1977?
7. Which of their albums was called by *New Musical Express* 'one of the most extreme, relentless, harrowing and downright iconoclastic pieces of music to have been made available this side of the sun'?
8. Where was 'Dark Side Of The Moon' first performed live in its entirety?
9. In which year did they begin their final tour in Miami?
10. Which session singer and songwriter co-wrote *The Great Gig In the Sky* with Rick Wright, but only received a credit on pressings of the record after she sued successfully for royalties?

Answers

1. *See Emily Play*
2. Roger Waters

3. The Countdown
4. Because of its references to cross-dressing
5. 14-hour Technicolor Dream
6. Nick Mason
7. 'Animals'
8. Rainbow Theatre, London
9. 1994
10. Clare Torry

Deep Purple

1. When Ritchie Blackmore and Jon Lord originally formed Roundabout, the group which later became Deep Purple, in 1968, the original vocalist was Chris Curtis, formerly drummer with which successful group?
2. When they signed to EMI in 1968, on which label did they release their first records prior to the formation of the Harvest label a year later?
3. Which Joe South song became their first US hit, though it did not chart in the UK until they re-recorded it twenty years later?
4. *Smoke On the Water* was written in 1971 about a casino which burned down in which Swiss town?
5. Which non-album track single, the follow-up to *Black Night*, was a UK Top 10 hit in spring 1971?
6. Who replaced Ian Gillan as vocalist in 1973?
7. What was the title of the TV-advertised compilation album which topped the UK chart in 1980?
8. Which was the second UK single from the 1984 album 'Perfect Strangers', which just made the Top 75 the following year?
9. Who joined the group as lead guitarist in 1975, replacing Ritchie Blackmore, but died from a heroin overdose shortly after they disbanded a year later?
10. What was the title of their live album released in 1988?

Answers

1. The Searchers
2. Parlophone
3. *Hush*
4. Montreux
5. *Strange Kind Of Woman*
6. David Coverdale
7. 'Deepest Purple'
8. *Knocking At Your Back Door*
9. Tommy Bolin
10. 'Nobody's Perfect'

Eric Clapton

1. Which band, in which Tom McGuinness, later of Manfred Mann, was also a guitarist, did Clapton join in 1963?
2. Which Cream single did he co-write with George Harrison?
3. Which was the only track he wrote on the Blind Faith album?
4. With whom did he co-write the song *Layla*?
5. What was the title of his live album released in the summer of 1975?
6. Which fellow guitarist organised the Rainbow Concert, London, in January 1973, staged to help him try and overcome his drug dependency?
7. Which Bob Marley song gave him a US No. 1 and UK top ten hit in 1974?
8. Who produced the albums 'Behind The Sun' and 'August'?
9. Where did he play a benefit concert for the Countryside Alliance on 20 May 2006?
10. Where is the Crossroads Centre, his facility for those recovering from substance abuse?

Answers

1. The Roosters
2. *Badge*
3. *Presence Of The Lord*
4. Jim Gordon
5. *E.C. Was Here*
6. Pete Townshend

7. *I Shot The Sheriff*
8. Phil Collins
9. Highclere Castle
10. Antigua

Jimi Hendrix

1. Which French singer did The Jimi Hendrix Experience back at a gig at Paris Olympia in October 1966?
2. Which of the Jimi Hendrix Experience albums reached No. 2 in the UK in summer 1967, only to be held off No. 1 by The Beatles' 'Sergeant Pepper'?
3. On which of their singles in 1967 did Hendrix play harpsichord as well as guitar, with vocal backing by the Sweet Inspirations?
4. On which singer's BBC TV show in January 1969 did Hendrix suddenly stop playing *Hey Joe,* begin *Sunshine Of Your Love* as a tribute to the recently disbanded Cream, and receive a warning afterwards that he would never work for the BBC again?
5. At which festival did the group play their last gig together in June 1969?
6. Which live album, which made the UK and US Top 10 in 1970, included Billy Cox on bass guitar and Buddy Miles on drums?
7. Which track was released as a single and topped the UK charts a few weeks after Hendrix's death?
8. Which former manager of Hendrix was killed in a plane crash over France in 1973?
9. Which single originally made the UK Top 40 in 1969, and was a minor Top 75 hit when reissued in 1990 after being used with a Wrangler TV commercial?

10. Which album, released in March 1971, contained the last studio recordings he ever made?

Answers

1. Johnny Hallyday
2. 'Are You Experienced'
3. *The Burning Of The Midnight Lamp*
4. Lulu
5. Denver Pop Festival
6. 'Band Of Gypsys'
7. *Voodoo Chile*
8. Michael Jeffery
9. *Crosstown Traffic*
10. 'Cry Of Love'

Free and Bad Company

1. Which group did guitarist David Kossoff and drummer Simon Kirke leave to help form Free in 1968?
2. On which 1970 album did the full-length version of *All Right Now* first appear?
3. After Free disbanded in 1971 and Paul Rodgers formed new group Peace, whom did they support on a UK tour?
4. Which guitarist from Osibisa joined them on a temporary basis for their final UK tour?
5. In which year did a three-track EP of Free hits reach No. 11 in the UK?
6. Who was the former King Crimson bass guitarist who joined Bad Company?
7. Who owned the mobile studio in which Bad Company recorded their first album?
8. Which track from the first album was a Top 20 single in the US though not released as such in the UK?
9. Which track from the album 'Straight Shooter' was a US Top 10 and UK Top 20 hit later in 1975?
10. Which was the final album they released in 1982 before the departure of Paul Rodgers?

Answers

1. Black Cat Bones
2. 'Fire And Water'

3. Mott The Hoople
4. Wendell Richardson
5. 1978
6. Boz Burrell
7. Ronnie Lane
8. *Movin' On*
9. *Feel Like Makin' Love*
10. 'Rough Diamonds'

Marvin Gaye

1. With which singer did Gaye duet on *Ain't Nothing Like the Real Thing* and *You're All I Need to Get By*?
2. Which was his first US Top 50 hit, reaching No. 46 in 1962?
3. He released a tribute album in November 1965 consisting of songs originally made famous by which performer who had died earlier that year?
4. *Wherever I Lay My Hat*, originally on the B-side of his 1969 hit *Too Busy Thinking About My Baby*, became a No. 1 hit for which British singer in 1983?
5. Which single was a US No. 1 and UK Top 10 hit for him in 1977?
6. Which member of the Four Tops, after witnessing an incident involving police brutality, co-wrote the title track of 'What's Going On' with Gaye?
7. *I Heard It Through The Grapevine* was a Top 10 UK hit again in May 1986 after being used to advertise what product on TV?
8. Who co-wrote the 1982 hit *Sexual Healing*, and also wrote the biography of Gaye, *Divided Soul*, published a year after his death?
9. Which album, consisting partly of standards like *Fly Me to the Moon* and *The Shadow of Your Smile*, was released in November 1985 although it failed to chart?
10. At which British venue did he record a mainly live album in October 1976, released the

following year (and also featuring the answer to No. 5, the only studio track)?

Answers

1. Tammi Terrell
2. *Stubborn Kind of Fellow*
3. Nat 'King' Cole
4. Paul Young
5. *Got To Give It Up*
6. Renaldo 'Obie' Benson
7. Levi jeans
8. David Ritz
9. 'Romantically Yours'
10. London Palladium

Stevie Wonder

1. Which Bob Dylan song gave Wonder a minor hit in 1966?
2. How old was he when he first signed to Motown Records?
3. What was the name of his 1977 hit which paid tribute to Duke Ellington?
4. With whom did he co-write the hits *I Was Made To Love Her*, *Uptight (Everything's Alright)* and *My Cherie Amour*?
5. What was the title of the Ray Charles tribute album he released in 1962?
6. Who was the singer and former Motown secretary whom he married in 1970?
7. In the 1980s, which of his hits went on to become the best-selling Motown single in the UK of all time?
8. On which Eurythmics hit did he play harmonica?
9 Which jazz musician is featured playing trumpet on the full 10-minuite version of *Do I Do*?
10. Which UK group had a minor hit in 1982 with *Living For the City*?

Answers

1. *Blowin' In The Wind*
2. 11
3. Sir Duke
4. Henry Cosby
5. 'Tribute to Uncle Ray'

6. Syreeta Wright
7. *I Just Called To Say I Love You*
8. *There Must Be An Angel (Playing With My Heart)*
9. Dizzy Gillespie
10. Gillan

Otis Redding

1. Which group, led by guitarist Johnny Jenkins, did Redding join as vocalist in 1958?
2. With whom did he co-write *(Sittin' On) The Dock of the Bay*?
3. What was the title of the last album he completed and released before his death, consisting of duets with Carla Thomas?
4. Which of his hits did he co-write with Jerry Butler of the First Impressions?
5. Which single gave him a posthumous UK Top 20 hit in the summer of 1968, and was also a hit for the Black Crowes in 1990?
6. Which member of the Bar-Kays was the sole survivor of the plane crash in which Otis was killed?
7. Which Beatles song gave him a Top 50 UK hit earlier in 1967?
8. Which of his albums, excluding compilations, included *Respect* and his version of *(I Can't Get No) Satisfaction*?
9. Which track on the album 'Love Man', released in 1969, was later to be a hit for Jackie Wilson under a slightly different title?
10. Which bass guitarist with Booker T. and the MGs was also a regular session musician on several of his recordings?

Answers

1. The Pinetoppers
2. Steve Cropper

3. 'King and Queen'
4. *I've Been Loving You Too Long*
5. *Hard To Handle*
6. Ben Cauley
7. *Day Tripper*
8. 'Otis Blue'
9. *(Your Love Has Lifted Me) Higher and Higher*
10. Donald 'Duck' Dunn

Van Morrison

1. Which song, probably Morrison's best-known, was a US Top 10 hit for him late in 1967, and a minor UK hit in 2013?
2. For which UK group was a cover version of *Jackie Wilson Says (I'm in Heaven When You Smile)* a UK top five hit in 1982?
3. With which pop/jazz performer did he record 'How Long Has This Been Going On' in 1995?
4. Which album did he record and release with the Chieftains in 1988?
5. Which was his first UK chart single, albeit reaching only No. 65 in 1979?
6. Which album did he record and release in 2000 with Linda Gail Lewis?
7. Which song, recorded with John Lee Hooker, gave him a UK Top 40 hit in 1993?
8. Which compilation reached No. 2 in the UK album chart in 2007?
9. At which venue did he perform the entire 'Astral Weeks' album live at two shows in November 2008?
10. Which album did he release in 1977 after a three-year silence since its predecessor?

Answers

1. *Brown-Eyed Girl*
2. Kevin Rowland and Dexy's Midnight Runners
3. Georgie Fame
4. 'Irish Heartbeat'
5. *The Bright Side of the Road*

6. 'You Win Again'
7. *Gloria*
8. 'Still on Top'
9. Hollywood Bowl, Los Angeles
10. 'A Period of Transition'

Neil Diamond

1. Which Monkees' transatlantic chart-topper, a hit in 1967, was written by Diamond?
2. Which was his first US No. 1, and became his first UK hit, reaching No. 3 in 1970?
3. At which venue did he record the live album 'Hot August Night' in August 1972, released five months later?
4. Which Gary U.S. Bonds rock'n'roll standard from 1960 gave him a minor US hit in 1968, the first cover version he ever recorded as a single?
5. With whom did he record the 1978/9 Top 10 hit duet, *You Don't Bring Me Flowers*?
6. Which of his albums made the US Top 10 and UK Top 50 late in 1982?
7. Who wrote and previously recorded *Until It's Time For You To Go*, a minor US hit for him in 1970?
8. In which movie did he star in 1979, opposite Sir Laurence Olivier, and provide the soundtrack music?
9. Which track gave him a US Top 30 hit in 1969 and was on the B-side of the UK hit *Sweet Caroline* in 1971?
10. Who produced his albums '12 Songs' and his first UK No. 1 album 'Home Before Dark'?

Answers

1. *I'm a Believer*
2. Cracklin' Rosie
3. The Greek Theater, Los Angeles

4. *New Orleans*
5. Barbra Streisand
6. ‘Heartlight’
7. Buffy Sainte-Marie
8. *The Jazz Singer*
9. *Brother Love’s Travelling Salvation Show*
10. Rick Rubin

Bob Seger

1. Which was Seger's first album to chart in the UK, reaching the Top 40 in 1978, also appearing on silver vinyl and as a picture disc?
2. At which venue was the album 'Live Bullet' recorded in September 1975?
3. Which British group made their UK Top 50 debut with 'Live at the Marquee' EP, including their version of Seger's *Get Out of Denver*, in 1976?
4. When Robyn Robbins left The Silver Bullet band in the late 1970s, which ex-Grand Funk Railroad member replaced him on keyboards?
5. Which Seger song did Thin Lizzy cover on their 1975 album 'Fighting', and also in a medley with *Cowgirl Song* on the 1978 'Live and Dangerous' set, giving them a Top 20 UK single that same year?
6. *We've Got Tonight* first made the UK Top 50 in 1978 and a live version also charted in 1982, but in which year did the original finally make the Top 30 when reissued to promote the 'Greatest Hits' album?
7. Who wrote his 1983 US No. 2 hit *Shame on the Moon*?
8. Which live track from 'Nine Tonight' gave him a US top five hit in 1981?
9. *Shakedown*, which in 1987 became his only US No. 1 single, came from the soundtrack of which movie?
10. On John Fogerty's album 'Wrote a Song for Everyone', which on which Fogerty composition did he and Seger duet?

Answers

1. 'Stranger in Town'
2. The Cobo Arena, Detroit
3. Eddie and the Hot Rods
4. Craig Frost
5. *Rosalie*
6. 1995
7. Rodney Crowell
8. *Tryin' to Lve My Life Without You*
9. 'Beverly Hills Cop'
10. *Who'll Stop the Rain*

Tina Turner

1. What is Tina Turner's original name?
2. Which Ike and Tina Turner single, produced by Phil Spector, reached No. 3 in the UK in 1966 but barely made the US Top 100?
3. Which British guitarist allegedly played on *Nutbush City Limits* in 1973?
4. Which role did Tina play in the movie version of The Who's *Tommy*?
5. Who had the original hit version of *Let's Stay Together*, which was her comeback single in 1983?
6. Who wrote *Private Dancer* for her?
7. With whom did she duet on the 1997 hit *In Your Wildest Dreams*?
8. Which song, which had been a hit the previous year for The Jacksons with Mick Jagger, did she perform with the latter at Live Aid, Philadelphia, in 1985?
9. For which Disney film did she record *Great Spirits* with Phil Collins in 2003?
10. Which 1985 Top 30 hit was a duet between her and Bryan Adams?

Answers

1. Annie Mae Bullock
2. *River Deep, Mountain High*
3. Marc Bolan
4. The Acid Queen
5. Al Green
6. Mark Knopfler

7. Barry White
8. *State Of Shock*
9. *Brother Bear*
10. *It's Only Love*

Fairport Convention

1. Who was the original vocalist, who left after the release of their first album in 1968?
2. What was their only British hit single, reaching No. 21 in 1969?
3. Which early album included the original version of their perennial stage favourite *Meet On the Ledge*?
4. Which short-lived group did Sandy Denny form in 1970 after leaving Fairport Convention with Trevor Lucas, Gerry Conway, Jerry Donahue and Pat Donaldson?
5. Which village in Oxfordshire has given its name to their festival held annually since August 1976?
6. On which label was their debut single *If I Had a Ribbon Bow* released in 1968?
7. Which early member left to form his own group, which included his name in their title and had a No. 1 single in 1970 with *Woodstock*?
8. Which of their drummers was tragically killed in a road accident in 1969?
9. 'Unhalfbricking' was one of only two Top 10 British albums for them; which was the other?
10. What was the title of their 40th anniversary album in 2007?

Answers

1. Judy Dyble
2. *Si Tu Dois Partir*
3. 'What We Did On Our Holidays

4. Fotheringay
5. Cropredy
6. Track
7. Ian Matthews
8. Martin Lamble
9. 'Angel Delight'
10. 'A Sense Of Occasion'

Steeleye Span

1. From the lyrics of which traditional song did the group originally take their name?
2. Which Irish husband and wife team were part of the group's original line-up but left in 1970 after they had completed recording the first album?
3. Which well-respected traditional folksinger and guitarist joined them in 1970, left a year later, and briefly rejoined them in 1977?
4. Which acappella Latin carol provided them with their first hit single in 1973?
5. Who produced the albums 'All Around my Hat' and 'Rocket Cottage'?
6. On which track on 'Commoners Crown', also an unsuccessful single, did Peter Sellers appear on guest vocals and ukulele?
7. When drummer Nigel Pegrum left in 1989, which musician replaced him?
8. Maddy Prior was awarded which official honour in 2001?
9. With which author did they collaborate on the album 'Wintersmith', released in 2013?
10. Which album did they release in 2016?

Answers

1. *Horkstow Grange*
2. Terry and Gay Woods
3. Martin Carthy
4. *Gaudete*
5. Mike Batt
6. *New York Girls*

7. Liam Genockey
8. MBE (Member of the British Empire)
9. Terry Pratchett
10. Dodgy Bastards

Emerson, Lake and Palmer
(and associated groups)

1. The Nice started out as a backing group for which soul singer, who had a solo UK Top 20 hit in 1967?
2. Released in 1972, which was ELP's only UK No. 1 album?
3. At which venue in March 1971 did they record their first live album, 'Pictures at an Exhibition', released in eight months later?
4. Who wrote *Fanfare for the Common Man*, their rearrangement of which gave them their only major UK hit in 1977?
5. Which was the only single released by Emerson, Lake and Powell from their self-titled 1986 album, and a minor hit in the US though it failed in the UK?
6. Emerson and Lake teamed up with which drummer to form the trio named 3, who released the album 'To the Power of Three' in 1988?
7. Which track from the first ELP album was never released as a single in the UK, though it gave them a Top 50 hit in the US?
8. Asia, the group Carl Palmer joined in 1981, made the UK top five album with their second album in 1983; what was the title?
9. Which track by ELP was initially released only on a give-away flexidisc with *New Musical*

Express in November 1973, and later as the B-side to *Fanfare for the Common Man*?
10. Where did ELP play a one-off anniversary gig, headlining the High Voltage Festival, in July 2010, later released on CD as 'High Voltage'?

Answers

1. P.P. Arnold
2. 'Tarkus'
3. Newcastle City Hall
4. Aaron Copland
5. Touch and Go
6. Robert Berry
7. *Lucky Man*
8. 'Alpha'
9. *Brain Salad Surgery*
10. Victoria Park, London

The Carpenters

1. Which was the duo's first minor US hit, a cover of a Beatles' song, which made the Top 60 in May 1970?
2. Which Bacharach-David song gave them their first UK Top 10 hit and US No. 1, later in 1970?
3. When they played at the White House in May 1974 at the request of President Nixon, which European statesman was being honoured at the state dinner that evening?
4. Who originally had a US No. 1 in 1961 with *Please Mr Postman*, which the duo also took to No. 1 and to No. 2 in the UK in 1975?
5. Which Herman's Hermits oldie gave them a transatlantic Top 30 hit in the spring of 1976?
6. Which Canadian group recorded the original version of *Calling Occupants of Interplanetary Craft (The Recognized Anthem of World Contact Day),* their transatlantic 1977 Top 40 hit?
7. When they recorded an ABC-TV Special, *Music, Music, Music* in 1980, with whom did Karen Carpenter duet on *This Masquerade*?
8. Which Paul Simon song appeared on Karen's solo album, originally recorded between 1979 and 1982 and rejected, remaining unreleased until 1996?
9. At which educational institution did Karen make her last singing appearance, in December 1982?
10. What was the title of Richard Carpenter's debut solo album, released in October 1987?

Answers

1. *Ticket to Ride*
2. *Close to You*
3. Willy Brandt, German Chancellor
4. The Marvelettes
5. *There's a Kind of Hush*
6. Klaatu
7. Ella Fitzgerald
8. *Still Crazy After All These Years*
9. Buckley School, Sherman Oaks, California
10. *Time*

Led Zeppelin

1. Which track was briefly released as a single from the group's first album in Britain and then withdrawn?
2. Which guest vocalist appeared on *The Battle Of Nevermore*?
3. In 1969, Sandie Shaw became the first artist to record and release a cover version of one of the group's songs – which one?
4. Which of their songs became a Top 10 hit for Far Corporation in the 1980s and Rolf Harris in the 1990s?
5. Who played piano on the *Physical Graffiti* album track *Boogie With Stu*?
6. What was the name of the film recorded at three shows at Madison Square Gardens in 1973?
7. On which single by Roy Wood, released in 1978, did John Bonham play drums?
8. What was the name of their album of out-takes, released in 1982?
9. In whose memory did the reformed band play a tribute concert in 2007 at the O_2 Arena?
10. Where did they record their final album *In Through The Out Door*?

Answers

1. *Communication Breakdown*
2. Sandy Denny
3. *Your Time is Gonna Come*
4. *Stairway To Heaven*

5. Ian Stewart
6. *The Song Remains the Same*
7. *Keep Your Hands On The Wheel*
8. *Coda*
9. Ahmet Ertegun
10. Polar Studios, Stockholm

Hot Chocolate

1. Which John Lennon song did they record as their furst single, under the name Hot Chocolate Band, and release on the Apple label in 1969?
2. On which record label did all their subsequent releases (barring reissues) appear in the UK?
3. Their first few hits were written by group members Errol Brown and Tom Wilson. Which instrument did the latter play in the line-up?
4. Which song written by the Brown-Wilson partnership became a Top 30 hit for Herman's Hermits in 1970?
5. Which of their hits, a Top 10 UK hit in 1973, featured Alexis Korner proving a brief spoken interlude, and became a No. 1 in the US when covered by the group Stories?
6. Which songwriter provided them in 1977 with their only No. 1 hit, *So You Win Again*?
7. Which of their hits originally made the top five in 1982, and on subsequent reissues the Top 40 in 1993 and the Top 20 in 1998?
8. *You Sexy Thing* had a new lease of life over twenty years after its first chart appearance when it was featured on the soundtrack of which film in 1997?
9. What was the title of their 1982 album, which reached No. 24 in the chart?
10. Which solo single by Errol Brown was a Top 30 hit in 1987?

Answers

1. *Give Peace a Chance*
2. RAK
3. Bass guitar
4. *Bet Yer Life I Do*
5. *Brother Louie*
6. Russ Ballard
7. *It Started With a Kiss*
8. *The Full Monty*
9. 'Mystery'
10. *Personal Touch*

David Bowie

1. Under what name were Bowie and his band credited on his debut 1964 single *Liza Jane*?
2. What was the title of the single he wrote for Oscar (later actor Paul Nicholas), released in 1967?
3. Which female singer had a top three hit in the UK 1974 with *The Man Who Sold the World*, on which he played saxophone, guitar and sang backing vocals?
4. Which single was belatedly released from the album 'Hunky Dory' to become a UK Top 3 hit in the summer of 1973?
5. Who produced the 'Let's Dance' album?
6. Which Beach Boys single did he cover on the 'Tonight' album?
7. Which group, lasting for two albums, did he form in 1989 with Reeves Gabrels, Tony and Hunt Sales?
8. For which TV crime drama series, shown in November 2015, did he write and record the opening title song?
9. At the Freddie Mercury tribute at Wembley Stadium in April 1992 (where he recited the Lord's Prayer on stage), with whom did he duet on *Under Pressure*?
10. What was the name of the character he played in the Christopher Nolan film *Prestige* in 2006?

Answers

1. Davie Jones with the King Bees
2. *Over The Wall We Go*
3. Lulu
4. *Life On Mars?*
5. Nile Rodgers
6. *God Only Knows*
7. Tin Machine
8. *Black Panthers*
9. Annie Lennox
10. Nikola Tesla

Queen

1. What was Queen's first, unsuccessful, single in the summer of 1973?
2. Which No. 1 single of 1981 was credited jointly to Queen and David Bowie?
3. At which venue did they play a gig on Christmas Eve 1975, televised live by the BBC?
4. Under which name did Freddie Mercury record and release a cover version of *I Can Hear Music* in 1973?
5. Which was the first of their hit singles written by John Deacon?
6. On 'The Works' tour, which additional musician played keyboards?
7. Which member played on Holly Johnson's *Love Train* and Living In A Box's *Blow The House Down*?
8. Which group did they support on tour in 1974?
9. Where was a statue of Freddie Mercury unveiled in 1996?
10. What was the name of Roger Taylor's band which recorded the albums 'Shove It' and 'Mad, Bad And Dangerous To Know'?

Answers

1. *Keep Yourself Alive*
2. *Under Pressure*
3. Hammersmith Odeon
4. Larry Lurex
5. *You're My Best Friend*

6. Spike Edney
7. Brian May
8. Mott The Hoople
9. Montreux, overlooking Lake Geneva
10. The Cross

Status Quo

1. Which single did an early version of the group release in 1967 under the name The Traffic Jam?
2. Which drummer replaced John Coghlan in 1982?
3. Which song by Bachman-Turner Overdrive did they cover on the 2003 album 'Riffs'?
4. Which was their last album to be released on the Vertigo label in 1991?
5. Which Beatles song did they (or rather Francis Rossi and an orchestra) perform on *All This And World War II* soundtrack?
6. Which of their hits contains the line 'But there ain't no room for a kosher cowboy in a town like New Orleans'?
7. Who played piano on their 1974 hit *Break the Rules*?
8. John Edwards and Jeff Rich were part of the band behind a female singer who had a Top 10 album in 1980 with 'Sports Car' – who?
9. Which writer collaborated with Rossi and Parfitt on their 2004 autobiography *XS All Areas*?
10. Jacqui Sullivan was one of the backing vocalists on the 1978 album 'If You Can't Stand The Heat' – of which successful group was she later a member?

Answers

1. *Almost But Not Quite There*
2. Peter Kircher

3. *Takin' Care Of Business*
4. 'Rock 'Til You Drop'
5. *Getting Better*
6. *Down The Dustpipe*
7. John Parker
8. Judie Tzuke
9. Mick Wall
10. Bananarama

T. Rex and Marc Bolan

1. What was the A-side of Bolan's first single on Decca, released in November 1965?
2. *Desdemona*, a single in 1967 by Bolan's group at the time, was banned by the BBC. Which was the group?
3. Excluding the 1972 reissues, which Tyrannosaurus Rex album reached the highest position in the UK charts, No. 12 in 1969?
4. Who was Bolan's original partner in Tyrannosaurus Rex, replaced by Mickey Finn in 1969?
5. When T. Rex appeared on *Top Of The Pops* promoting *Get It On*, who joined them on (well, miming) piano?
6. On which female singer's BBC TV show did Bolan appear in 1973, duetting on *Life's a Gas*?
7. Which was the first T. Rex hit single to be released on the T. Rex label?
8. Which former member of CCS and Blue Mink, and future member of Sky, played bass guitar with T. Rex from August 1976 until Bolan's death?
9. Which single entered the UK charts at No. 3 on its initial release in 1973 and reappeared in the Top 20 on reissue in 1991?
10. Which punk group opened for T. Rex on the latter's final tour starting in March 1977?

Answers

1. *The Wizard*
2. John's Children
3. 'Unicorn'
4. Steve Peregrine Took
5. Elton John
6. Cilla Black
7. *Telegram Sam*
8. Herbie Flowers
9. *20th Century Boy*
10. The Damned

Slade

1. Which was the single released in December 1966 by the group when they were known as The In-Be-Tweens?
2. Which was their first UK No. 1 single, on which Jim Lea played violin?
3. When they began their first headlining tour in Britain at Bradford in May 1972, which group supported them?
4. Which was their third consecutive No. 1 album in the UK, released in February 1974?
5. In addition to bass guitar and keyboards, which wind instrument did Jim Lea play on *How Does It Feel*?
6. Which single by Girlschool, released in January 1984, was written and produced by Noddy Holder and Jim Lea?
7. On which label did their releases appear between 1977 and 1979?
8. At which major gig in August 1980 did the group make what was effectively their comeback, after having decided beforehand that they would probably disband afterwards?
9. Which US rock group had an American top five hit in 1983 with their version of *Cum On Feel The Noize*?
10. Which of their compilation albums, released in November 1991, included their last two singles *Radio Wall of Sound* and *Universe*?

Answers

1. *You Better Run*
2. *Coz I Luv You*
3. Status Quo
4. *'Old, New, Borrowed and Blue'*
5. Flute
6. *Burning in the Heat*
7. Barn
8. Reading Rock Festival
9. Quiet Riot
10. 'Wall of Hits'

Lindisfarne

1. After originally calling themselves Downtown Faction, what name did they choose briefly before settling on Lindisfarne, before having to alter it in order to avoid confusion with an American act?
2. Which song from the first album took as its title (which does not appear in the lyric) a parody from a track on the Beatles' 'Sergeant Pepper' album?
3. Which American producer, who had also helmed albums by Bob Dylan, Leonard Cohen, and Simon & Garfunkel, produced their second and third albums 'Fog on the Tyne' and 'Dingly Dell'?
4. When they appeared on *Top of the Pops* promoting *Meet Me on the Corner* in 1972, with what did Ray Laidlaw hit the bass drum?
5. On which label in Britain did they release the album Happy Daze in 1974?
6. Which of their hits went on to become their only Top 40 success in America?
7. At which venue in Newcastle did they play in the summer of 1984 on the same bill as Bob Dylan and Santana?
8. Which saxophonist and flautist made the group a six-piece when he joined in the mid-1980s?
9. Which member left the group in 1994 to run a brewery in Canada?
10. Which song co-written by Rod Clements and Nigel Stonier originally appeared on their 1998 album 'Here Comes the Neighbourhood' in 1998, and was a Top 30 hit for Erin Rocha five years later?

Answers

1. Brethren
2. *Alan in the River With Flowers*
3. Bob Johnston
4. A rubber fish
5. Warner Brothers
6. Run For Home
7. St James' Park
8. Marty Craggs
9. Si Cowe
10. *Can't Do Right For Doing Wrong*

10cc

1. Which Graham Gouldman song became a Top 10 hit for Herman's Hermits in 1966?
2. Kevin Godley and Lol Creme released *I'm Beside Myself* on the Marmalade label in 1969, under what name?
3. Which record did they take to No. 2 in the summer of 1970 under the name Hotlegs?
4. What was their unsuccessful single follow-up to *Donna* at the end of 1972?
5. Where did they play the opening gig of their first British tour in August 1973?
6. What was the title of their 1977 live double album?
7. With which American singer-songwriter did Graham Gouldman form the 1980s duo Wax?
8. Which triple album did Kevin Godley and Lol Creme record shortly after leaving the group in 1976?
9. Which group did they support at Knebworth in August 1976?
10. Who replaced Kevin Godley on drums?

Answers

1. *No Milk Today*
2. Frabjoy and Runcible
3. *Neanderthal Man*
4. *Johnny Don't Do It*
5. Douglas Palace Lido, Isle of Man
6. 'Live And Let Live'
7. Andrew Gold

8. ‘Consequences’
9. The Rolling Stones
10. Paul Burgess

Elton John

1. Which Elton John track, previously released on 'Goodbye Yellow Brick Road', became a No. 1 US hit single in 1974, but only made the UK Top 40 on belated release in September 1976?
2. Under which assumed names did he and Bernie Taupin credit themselves as songwriters on his first UK chart-topper *Don't Go Breaking My Heart*?
3. Who directed the video for *Nikita?*
4. Which modestly-selling disco album, reaching only No. 41 in the UK, did he release in 1979?
5. Who produced the 1979 US hit *Mama Can't Buy You Love*?
6. When *Sacrifice* was reissued to become a No. 1 UK single in 1990, it was a double A-side with which other track, a year after which both had separately been only minor hits?
7. With which lyricist did he collaborate on songs for the Disney animated film *The Lion King* in 1994?
8. Which British female vocalist, who had several hits in the 1960s, sang backing vocals on *The Bitch Is Back*?
9. At which New York City venue did he perform for the 60th time to celebrate his 60th birthday in 1997?
10. With which American performer did he record the 2010 album 'Union'?

Answers

1. *Bennie And The Jets*
2. Ann Orson and Carte Blanche (orson carte, geddit?)
3. Ken Russell
4. *'Victim Of Love'*
5. Thom Bell
6. *Healing Hands*
7. Tim Rice
8. Dusty Springfield
9. Madison Square Gardens
10. Leon Russell

Steve Winwood

1. Which Spencer Davis Group hit was co-written by Steve with his brother Muff and Spencer Davis?
2. Who was the Spencer Davis Group producer with whom Steve wrote their last hit *I'm a Man*?
3. The success of *Keep On Running* enabled Steve to buy which instrument?
4. Which Traffic single, their third, was made for the soundtrack of which film of the same title?
5. Which Traffic album reached the US Top 10 in 1971, but did not chart in the UK?
6. On which solo album did his first solo hit *While You See a Chance* first appear?
7. Which album released in 1994 was largely a solo recording, but still released as a new album by Traffic?
8. With which guitarist, with whom he had worked before, did he play three sold-out shows at Madison Square Garden in February 2008?
9. After Blind Faith disbanded in 1969, he stayed with Ric Grech to join which new but similarly shortlived group?
10. Which Top 20 hit in 1983 by Will Powers, with uncredited vocal by Carly Simon, did he co-write?

Answers

1. *Gimme Some Lovin'*
2. Jimmy Miller
3. Hammond B-3 organ

4. *Here We Go Round The Mulberry Bush*
5. 'The Low Spark Of High-Heeled Boys'
6. 'Arc Of A Diver'
7. 'Far From Home'
8. Eric Clapton
9. Ginger Baker's Air Force
10. *Kissing With Confidence*

Roy Wood

1. On which record label, first formed in 1932 and reactivated in 1967, did four of The Move's singles and their first two albums appear?
2. At which London venue did Wizzard make their live debut on the star-studded Rock'n'Roll Show in August 1972?
3. Who played bass guitar with The Move from 1969 to 1971, again with Wizzard, and subsequently played pedal steel guitar with the Wizzo Band?
4. Which track was released as a Move single in May 1971 but withdrawn almost immediately in favour of the more commercial *Tonight*?
5. Which studio engineer played harmonium on *Songs of Praise*, the first track on Roy's album 'Boulders'?
6. What was the sub-title of Roy's 1974 solo hit *Goin' Down the Road*?
7. Which was the Move's final Top 10 hit, in the summer of 1972?
8. What was the name of the solo album by Annie Haslam of Renaissance, on which Roy played most of the instruments in addition to producing?
9. What was Roy's first solo single, released in January 1972?
10. Which album by Roy Wood's Wizzard was belatedly released as a CD on the Edsel label in 2000?

Answers

1. Regal Zonophone
2. Wembley Arena
3. Rick Price
4. *Ella James*
5. John Kurlander
6. A Scottish Reggae Song
7. *California Man*
8. 'Annie in Wonderland'
9. *When Gran'ma Plays the Banjo*
10. 'Main Street'

The Bee Gees

1. What was the name of the skiffle group the brothers formed in the 1950s while at school in Manchester?
2. Which former child actor was the group's drummer until 1969?
3. Which song was a Top 10 American hit for them in 1975 and a Top 10 hit for Candi Staton in Britain two years later?
4. Which label was formed by their manager, and released all their new material from 1973 to 1983?
5. Which was the group's last Top 20 single and title track of their final studio album in 2001?
6. In 1968 they had a British Top 30 hit with a double A-side. One track was *Jumbo*; what was the other?
7. Which member of the group had a No. 2 solo hit in 1969 with *Saved By the Bell*?
8. Which of their chart-topping singles later became a British No. 1 in 1998 for Steps?
9. Who presented the TV show on which the group suddenly terminated an interview in 1997 by walking off because they apparently took offence at his remarks?
10. Which No. 1 single for Diana Ross was co-written and co-produced by the group?

Answers

1. The Rattlesnakes
2. Colin Petersen

3. *Nights On Broadway*
4. RSO Records
5. *This Is Where I Came In*
6. *The Singer Sang His Song*
7. Robin Gibb
8. *Tragedy*
9. Clive Anderson
10. *Chain Reaction*

The Stranglers

1. When Hugh Cornwell formed Emil and the Detectives, a covers group while at William Ellis School, Highgate in the mid-1960s, he played bass guitar; which future renowned singer-songwriter played lead guitar?
2. Which American singer did The Stranglers support on their first major UK tour in September 1976?
3. For which BBC Radio 1 DJ did the group record their first live session in March 1977?
4. Which 1960s chart-topping hit was covered in 1977 by group and vocalist Celia Collin and credited to Celia and The Mutations?
5. Which 1979 album by the group was initially released with a limited edition 3D sleeve design?
6. What was the title of the book Hugh Cornwell wrote about his three-month prison sentence in 1980 for possession of drugs?
7. Released in 1983, which was the group's first album after they signed with the Epic label?
8. Which song, originally a hit for The Kinks, gave them a UK Top 10 hit in 1988?
9. Which former member of The Vibrators replaced Cornwell as vocalist in 1990?
10. Which single, released in 2004, became their first UK Top 40 hit for over thirteen years?

Answers

1. Richard Thompson

2. Patti Smith
3. John Peel
4. *Mony Mony*
5. 'The Raven'
6. *Inside Information*
7. 'Feline'
8. *All Day and All of the Night*
9. John Ellis
10. *Big Thing Coming*

The Sex Pistols

1. To which Alice Cooper song playing on the jukebox at Malcolm McLaren's shop did John Lydon allegedly mime as part of his audition for the group?
2. At which prison did they play a gig for inmates in September 1976?
3. Which other group, who were also signed to EMI, had originally been asked to appear on Thames TV's Today programme but had to pull out at the last moment, thus leaving the slot for the group for their notorious interview on 1 December 1976?
4. Which single topped the official UK singles chart in silver jubilee week, June 1977, when it was alleged that *God Save the Queen* had probably sold more copies?
5. Which ABBA single allegedly inspired the guitar riff which opens *Pretty Vacant*?
6. At which American venue did the group play their final gig in January 1978 before disbanding?
7. A cover version of which song first recorded by the Monkees gave the group a Top 30 UK hit in July 1980?
8. What was the title of the six-month tour which the four original members played on reforming in 1996?
9. Which group did Steve Jones and Paul Cook form in 1979?
10. What was the title of John Lydon's first book of memoirs, published in 1993?

Answers

1. *School's Out*
2. Chelmsford
3. Queen
4. *I Don't Want to Talk About It,* Rod Stewart
5. *S.O.S*
6. Winterland Ballroom, San Francisco
7. *(I'm Not Your) Stepping Stone*
8. The Filthy Lucre Tour
9. The Professionals
10. No Irish, No Blacks, No Dogs

AC/DC

1. Who did Cliff Williams replace in 1977 on bass guitar?
2. Who designed the group's logo in 1977?
3. Which minor UK hit for the group in 1979 was reissued in 2013 and became their first British Top 10 single when it entered the charts at No. 4?
4. Who joined the group on drums in 1983 and left to join Dio in 1989?
5. Which single in 1978 brought them their first appearance on *Top of The Pops* and was subsequently their first UK Top 30 hit, reaching No. 24?
6. At which event in Toronto in July 2003 did the group perform on the same bill as the Rolling Stones and Rush?
7. When Brian Johnson auditioned for the group in 1980 after the death of Bon Scott, which Ike and Tina Turner song did he sing?
8. In which city in Western Australia was Bon Scott buried, and a statue of him unveiled in October 2008?
9. What was the title of the group's live album released in November 2012?
10. Which movie, written and directed by Stephen King, used the group's 1986 album 'Who Made Who' for the soundtrack?

Answers

1. Mark Evans
2. Gerard Huerta

3. *Highway to Hell*
4. Simon Wright
5. *Rock'n'Roll Damnation*
6. Molson Canadian Rocks
7. *Nutbush City Limits*
8. Fremantle
9. 'Live at River Plate'
10. *Maximum Overdrive*

Lemmy and Motörhead

1. What was Lemmy's real name?
2. With which group from Blackpool did Lemmy play guitar between 1965 and 1967?
3. On which Hawkwind single, which reached No. 3 in 1972 and was a Top 40 hit again in 1978, did Lemmy sing lead vocal?
4. What was the title of Motörhead's first album, recorded for United Artists and completed in 1976 but not released until three years later?
5. Which group had a minor hit in 1981 with *Don't Do That*, featuring Lemmy, Cozy Powell on drums and two of the Nolan Sisters on backing vocals?
6. Which ZZ Top song became the title track of a Motörhead EP released on the Big Beat label in 1980?
7. Lemmy appeared alongside Gary Lineker in a TV advertisement for which product?
8. At which event did Motörhead play their final UK gig in June 2015?
9. Which live Motörhead album was released in 1981 and topped the UK album chart in its first week on sale?
10. Which former Motörhead drummer died in November, six weeks before Lemmy?

Answers

1. Ian Fraser Kilmister
2. The Rockin' Vickers
3. *Silver Machine*
4. 'On Parole'

5. The Young and Moody Band
6. *Beer Drinkers and Hell Raisers*
7. Walkers Crisps
8. Glastonbury Festival
9. 'No Sleep 'Til Hammersmith'
10. Phil 'Philthy Animal' Taylor

Meat Loaf

1. With which female singer did Meat Loaf record an album in 1970 for the Rare Earth label?
2. In which musical, based on a play by Shakespeare, did he play the priest at a production at the Minskoff Theater, New York, in 1976?
3. Which was the first hit single to be released in the UK from 'Bat Out Of Hell'?
4. With whom did he duet on the album track and UK Top 10 single *Dead Ringer For Love*?
5. Which Chuck Berry song did he cover on the 1983 album 'Midnight At The Lost And Found'?
6. What was the name of the group which Meat Loaf and Jim Steinman put together to back him on stage while touring 'Bat Out Of Hell'?
7. Who sang joint lead vocals on the title track of 'Bad Attitude'?
8. Which track from 'Blind Before I Stop' was recorded as a duet with John Parr and became a UK Top 40 single in 1986?
9. Lorraine Crosby sang backing vocals on *I'd Do Anything For Love (But I Won't Do That)* in 1993, but under what name was she credited on the record?
10. In which 1997 movie, staring a well-known British girl group of the time, did he make a brief appearance as a bus driver?

Answers

1. Stoney
2. *Rockabye Hamlet*
3. You Took The Words Right Out Of My Mouth
4. Cher
5. *Promised Land*
6. Neverland Express
7. Roger Daltrey
8. *Rock'n'Roll Mercenaries*
9. Mrs Loud
10. *Spiceworld: The Movie* (Spice Girls)

U2

1. At which Dublin school did U2 originally form in 1976?
2. Who became their manager shortly before they began recording?
3. After initially calling themselves Feedback, what name did they briefly adopt in 1977?
4. Who produced their first three albums?
5. What was the name of their live album, consisting of material performed on stage in Colorado and Sankt Goarshausen, Germany, released in November 1983?
6. Which of their singles, a Top 10 hit in 1989 and a track from the album 'Rattle And Hum', included the vocals and guitar of B.B. King?
7. Who was Bono's personal assistant and roadie, killed in an accident in July 1986?
8. Where is the Joshua tree, which inspired the album of the same name?
9. Which song on 'Rattle And Hum' was co-written by Bono and Bob Dylan?
10. Which charity benefited from the profits made on sales of their 1998 single *The Sweetest Thing*?

Answers

1. Mount Temple Comprehensive
2. Paul McGuinness
3. The Hype
4. Steve Lillywhite
5. 'Under A Blood Red Sky'

6. *When Love Comes To Town*
7. Greg Carroll
8. Mojave Desert, California
9. *Love Rescue Me*
10. Chernobyl Children's Project International

Michael Jackson and The Jackson Five

1. Who produced the album 'Thriller'?
2. What was Michael Jackson's first solo single, a US Top 10 hit in 1971 and UK Top 10 early the following year?
3. Apart from Michael, who was the only one of the Jackson brothers to have any solo hit singles in Britain?
4. With whom did he duet in 1982 on *The Girl Is Mine*?
5. At which London venue did he play seven sell-out concerts during the Bad tour in summer 1988?
6. Bill Bottrell played guitar on *Black Or White*, but which guitarist was initially credited mistakenly with having done so?
7. Which track on 'Bad' shares its name with a popular BBC TV situation comedy of the mid-1980s?
8. Which actress presented Michael Jackson with the Soul Train Heritage Award in 1989?
9. What was the name of his autobiography, published in 1988?
10. Who had a US No. 1 and UK No. 2 in 1992 with a cover of the Jackson 5's *I'll Be There*?

Answers

1. Quincy Jones
2. *Got To Be There*

3. Jermaine
4. Paul McCartney
5. Wembley Stadium
6. Slash
7. *Just Good Friends*
8. Elizabeth Taylor
9. *Moonwalk*
10. Mariah Carey

Bob Marley and The Wailers

1. Bob Marley and the Wailers had a double A-side hit towards the end of 1977 with *Jamming* and which other song?
2. Which singer had a UK hit with Bob's song *Stir It Up* in 1972?
3. At which London venue were the single *No Woman No Cry* and the album 'Live' recorded in 1975?
4. With which American singer were the group planning to go on tour in the US in the autumn of 1980 until it was cancelled after Bob collapsed in New York?
5. In which country did they play at the Independence Day celebrations in April 1980?
6. Who was the group's manager who was injured with Bob and his wife Rita in an attempt on Bob's life in Kingston in December 1976?
7. What was the title of the compilation LP which entered the UK charts at No. 1 on release in May 1984?
8. Who was The Wailers' drummer, shot dead outside his home in Kingston in 1987?
9. Which trio, including Rita Marley, provided backing vocals for the group from 1974 onwards?
10. Who did they support at a gig at Max's Kansas City, New York, in July 1973?

Answers

1. *Punky Reggae Party*
2. Johnny Nash
3. The Lyceum
4. Stevie Wonder
5. Zimbabwe
6. Don Taylor
7. 'Legend'
8. Carlton Barrett
9. The I-Threes
10. Bruce Springsteen

Lionel Richie and The Commodores

1. In which 1978 movie did The Commodores appear briefly, performing *Too Hot Ta Trot* during the dance contest?
2. Which Commodores album featured the hits *Flying High* and *Three Times a Lady*?
3. Which member of Toto played guitar on Richie's *Running With the Night*?
4. After Richie left The Commodores, which was their only transatlantic top five hit, reaching No.1 in the US and No.3 in the UK, without Richie?
5. Who replaced Richie in the Commodores in 1982 as lead vocalist?
6. Which single by Kenny Rogers, which topped the US chart in 1980, was written and produced by Richie?
7. What was the title of Richie's 2012 album, consisting of duets with country performers including Rogers, Shania Twain, Willie Nelson and Jimmy Buffett?
8. Which album by Richie stayed in the UK Top 10 throughout 1984 and was ultimately the biggest-selling album in Britain that year?
9. With whom did Richie duet on the 1981 hit *Endless Love*?
10. What was the title of the 1992 compilation album, featuring hits from the group and from Richie as a soloist?

Answers

1. *Thank God It's Friday*
2. 'Natural High'
3. Steve Lukather
4. *Nightshift*
5. Skyler Jett
6. *Lady*
7. 'Tuskegee'
8. 'Can't Slow Down'
9. Diana Ross
10. 'Back to Front'

Electric Light Orchestra

1. At which venue in Croydon did the group make their live debut on 16 April 1972?
2. On which record label, established by Don and David Arden in 1974, did all the group's new releases appear between 1977 and 1983?
3. Which instrument did Steve Woolam play on the group's first album, released in 1971?
4. 'Discovery' was the group's first British No. 1 album; which was the second (and last)?
5. Which opera diva sang the vocal introduction to *Rockaria!*?
6. At which studios in the Bahamas did the group record part of the album 'Balance Of Power' in 1985?
7. Which piece of classical music did they record on their album 'On The Third Day'?
8. Which new album was released under the name ELO in 2001, although it was in effect largely a Jeff Lynne solo album on which he was augmented by guest musicians?
9. Which member of the group wrote and published *The ELO Story* in 1980?
10. What title was officially given to the American release of the group's first album, allegedly owing to a misunderstanding when a secretary rang the English office to ask what it was?

Answers

1. The Greyhound
2. Jet
3. Violin
4. 'Time'
5. Mary Thomas
6. Compass Point, Nassau
7. *In The Hall Of The Mountain King*
8. ' Zoom'
9. Bev Bevan
10. 'No Answer'

Rod Stewart and the Faces

1. Rod Stewart's version of which Rolling Stones song appeared on side one, track one of his debut album 'An Old Raincoat'll Never Let You Down'?
2. Who was the mandolin player from Lindisfarne who played on all three of his solo albums between 1971 and 1974, although not credited by name on the first?
3. Who produced the album 'Atlantic Crossing'?
4. Which group did he join in 1965, which also included Peter Bardens and Beryl Marsden?
5. What was the full title of the Faces' live album released in 1974?
6. Whose spoken contributions were heard on the Small Faces' album 'Ogden's Nut Gone Flake'?
7. Which old Motown classic duet was a hit for Rod and Tina Turner in 1990?
8. Who replaced Ronnie Lane on bass in the Faces in 1973?
9. When *Sailing* was reissued as a charity record in 1987 and made the UK chart for the third time, which organisation benefited from the royalties?
10. Which track on 'Smiler' in 1974 was co-written by Elton John and includes him on vocals and piano?

Answers

1. *Street Fighting Man*
2. Ray Jackson
3. Tom Dowd
4. Shotgun Express
5. 'Coast To Coast: Overture And Beginners'
6. Stanley Unwin
7. *It Takes Two*
8. Tetsu Yamauchi
9. Zeebrugge Ferry Disaster Fund
10. *Let Me Be Your Car*

Bryan Ferry and Roxy Music

1. What was the name of the R'n'B outfit Bryan Ferry formed with Graham Simpson and John Porter while at university?
2. Which Roxy Music album (excluding compilations, obviously) included *Street Life, Song Of Europe* and *Mother Of Pearl*?
3. What was the B-side of *Love Is The Drug*?
4. Which John Lennon song did they record as a tribute after his death?
5. Jerry Hall appears on the cover of the album 'Siren', but on which island did the photoshoot take place?
6. Which member of Roxy Music released his first solo album 'Diamond Head' in 1975?
7. Which Joe South song did Ferry cover on his second solo album 'Another Time, Another Place' in 1974?
8. On which Roxy Music album does Ferry's girlfriend and future wife Lucy Helmore appear on the front cover, wearing a medieval helmet with a falcon perched on her gloved hand?
9. With which British retailer did Ferry sign a contract in 2006 to model their Autograph men's clothing range?
10. Who played guitar on Ferry's performance at Live Aid in 1985?

Answers

1. The Gas Board
2. 'Stranded'
3. *Sultanesque*
4. *Jealous Guy*
5. Anglesey
6. Phil Manzanera
7. *Walk A Mile In My Shoes*
8. 'Avalon'
9. Marks & Spencer
10. Dave Gilmour

Phil Collins and Genesis

1. Of which group had Phil Collins been a member before he joined Genesis in 1970?
2. What was the group's first single in 1968?
3. Which was the first album they recorded after Peter Gabriel's departure, with Collins on lead vocals?
4. Which group single topped the US chart in 1986, although it failed to make the UK Top 10?
5. Who was the former vocalist with Stiltskin who replaced Collins in 1997?
6. Which song, originally a hit for the Mindbenders in 1966, gave Collins a UK No. 1 in 1988?
7. Peter Fluck and Roger Law, the artists responsible for the satirical TV show *Spitting Image*, created the video for which of the group's singles?
8. What was the first solo album released by guitarist Steve Hackett?
9. Which jazz fusion-trained drummer played with them live on their 1977 tour?
10. What was the title of Collins's album of Motown covers, released in 2010?

Answers

1. Flaming Youth
2. *Silent Sun*
3. 'A Trick of the Tail'

4. *Invisible Touch*
5. Ray Wilson
6. *A Groovy Kind of Love*
7. *Land of Confusion*
8. 'Voyage of the Acolyte'
9. Chester Thompson
10. 'Going Back'

Dave Edmunds and Nick Lowe

1. Who played bass guitar with Dave Edmunds's first hit-making group Love Sculpture, later rejoined his band, and also wrote hits in the 1980s for Status Quo, Alvin Stardust, and Phil Everly with Cliff Richard?
2. At which pub in Kentish Town did Nick Lowe and his first major group Brinsley Schwarz have a residency in their early days?
3. What was Edmunds's first solo hit, which topped the UK charts for six weeks at the end of 1970?
4. What was Lowe's first solo single, not a hit, and the first single on the Stiff label in 1976?
5. Who wrote Edmunds's minor 1979 hit *Crawling From The Wreckage*?
6. What was the first hit by the Pretenders, produced by Nick?
7. Which former guitarist and subsequently bass guitarist with The Move wrote Dave's 1972 single *Down Down Down*?
8. Released in 1985, which was the final album to be credited to Nick Lowe and his Cowboy Outfit?
9. Which minor hit for Edmunds in 1983 was written and produced by Jeff Lynne?
10. Which group did Lowe form in the early 1990s also including John Hiatt, Jim Keltner and Ry Cooder?

Answers

1. John Williams (initially known by this name, but later as John David)
2. The Tally Ho
3. *I Hear You Knockin'*
4. *So It Goes*
5. Graham Parker
6. *Stop Your Sobbin'*
7. Trevor Burton
8. 'The Rose of England'
9. *Slipping Away*
10. Little Village

ABBA

1. Which of the group’s No. 1 singles had a title which could also be found in the lyrics of the record that immediately preceded it at the top of the chart?
2. Which veteran American singer collaborated with them on writing *Ring Ring*?
3. Which song was released from ‘ABBA - The Album’ as a single in 1978 and made the Top 10 in most European countries, but was never released as a single in the UK or US?
4. Of which group had Bjorn Ulvaeus been a member in the 1960s?
5. What was the group’s final album in 1981 before they disbanded?
6. Which single featured backing vocals on the final chorus from a children's choir?
7. *Angeleyes* was a double A-side in 1979 with which other track?
8. Who was the group’s manager, their co-lyricist on the earlier songs, and the founder of Polar Records?
9. Which was their only US No. 1 single, doing so in 1977?
10. Who had a Top 10 hit in 1974 with *Honey Honey*?

Answers

1. *Mamma Mia* (the previous chart-topper having been Queen’s *Bohemian Rhapsody*)
2. Neil Sedaka

3. *The Eagle*
4. Hootenanny Singers
5. 'The Visitors'
6. *I Have A Dream*
7. *Voulez-Vous*
8. Stig Anderson
9. *Dancing Queen*
10. Sweet Dreams

The Eagles

1. Which duo was formed by Glenn Frey and John David Souther in the late 1960s?
2. Who produced their first album in 1972?
3. Which song on the first album, with Don Henley on vocals, is thought to have been inspired partly by the story of Zelda Fitzgerald, and became the first US top ten single?
4. Which instrumental from the 'One of These Nights' album was later used as the theme music for the BBC radio and TV adaptations of *The Hitchhiker's Guide to the Galaxy*?
5. Which of their songs did Don Henley say was 'basically a song about the dark underbelly of the American Dream and about excess in America'?
6. Which member played bass guitar and left the group in 1977?
7. Which of their songs was co-written by Bob Seger, featured him on backing vocal, and was their last US No. 1?
8. Which track was released as a single from the album 'Eagles Live', and in 1980 became their last Top 30 US hit?
9. Which British musician and songwriter wrote the single *Love Will Keep Us Alive*, which also appeared on the mainly live album 'Hell Freezes Over'?
10. Which musician joined the band on guitars, mandolin, keyboards and backing vocals when they resumed touring in 2001, basically as a replacement for Don Felder?

Answers

1. Longbranch Pennywhistle
2. Glyn Johns
3. *Witchy Woman*
4. *Journey of the Sorcerer*
5. *Hotel California*
6. Randy Meisner
7. *Heartache Tonight*
8. *Seven Bridges Road*
9. Paul Carrack
10. Steuart Smith

Fleetwood Mac

1. On which shortlived label, part of CBS, was *Albatross* released as a single at the end of 1968?
2. Under which name was the group credited on *Somebody's Gonna Get Their Head Kicked in Tonite,* the B-side of the 1969 single *Man of the World*?
3. Which group did Peter Green leave in 1967 to help form Fleetwood Mac?
4. At which British festival did the group make their debut in August 1967?
5. Which album featured the hit singles *Little Lies*, *Seven Wonders*, and *Everywhere*?
6. Which was their only single from the album 'Rumours' to reach the UK Top 30?
7. Which female vocalist was rumoured in 2008 to be about to join the group as a replacement for Christine McVie, until various members issued a denial?
8. Which was their last hit with Peter Green, recorded early in 1970?
9. Which former member of the Idle Race and Savoy Brown joined the group in 1972?
10. Which member of the group recorded the solo albums 'Wild Heart' and 'Rock a Little' in the early 1980s?

Answers

1. Blue Horizon
2. Earl Vince and the Valiants

3. John Mayall and his Bluesbreakers
4. Windsor Jazz & Blues Festival
5. 'Tango in the Night'
6. *Dreams*
7. Sheryl Crow
8. *The Green Manalishi (with the Two-Pronged Crown)*
9. Dave Walker
10. Stevie Nicks

Kate Bush

1. Which track from 'The Kick Inside' did EMI initially want to be Bush's debut single, in preference to *Wuthering Heights*?
2. With whom did she duet on the 1986 top ten single *Don't Give Up*?
3. What was her festive Top 30 single in December 1980?
4. Which was her first album which she produced herself?
5. With which Elton John song did she have a Top 20 hit in 1991?
6. Her song *Flower of the Mountain* contains a passage from Molly Bloom's soliloquy in *Ulysses*, a novel by whom?
7. On which 1987 chart-topping charity single did she sing one line?
8. Which electropop duo invited her to produce one of their albums, although she declined because 'she didn't feel that that was her area'?
9. Which George Gershwin song did she cover in 1994 for the tribute album, 'The Glory of Gershwin'?
10. Who wrote a song for her, *Bird in Hand*, about the exploitation of parrots, which however she turned down?

Answers

1. *James and the Cold Gun*
2. Peter Gabriel
3. *December Will Be Magic Again*

4. 'The Dreaming'
5. *Rocket Man*
6. James Joyce
7. *Let it Be*, Ferry Aid
8. Erasure
9. *The Man I Love*
10. John Lydon (Johnny Rotten)

Madonna

1. What is Madonna's full real name?
2. Which band did she form with Dan Guitry in 1979, playing drums and guitar as well as singing?
3. The video for which single in 1989 was condemned by the Vatican for its use of Catholic symbols and imagery about a dream of making love to a saint?
4. Who produced her single *Holiday*?
5. She only had two UK No. 1 hits in the 1990s; one was *Vogue*, but what was the other?
6. Who did she marry on her birthday in 1985?
7. Which movie, in which she starred, included her first UK No. 1 *Into The Groove*?
8. What was the title of her first compilation album in 1990?
9. Which 1970s hit did she sample on *Hung Up* in 2005?
10. With which early 1970s classic song did she have a No. 1 in 2000?

Answers

1. Madonna Louise Ciccone
2. The Breakfast Club
3. *Like A Prayer*
4. John 'Jellybean' Benitez
5. *Frozen*
6. Sean Penn
7. *Desperately Seeking Susan*
8. *The Immaculate Collection*

9. *Gimme Gimme Gimme (A Man After Midnight),* ABBA
10. *American Pie*

Blondie

1. Who produced Blondie's eponymous album 'Blondie' and also the follow-up, 'Plastic Letters'?
2. Which British bass guitarist joined the group in 1977?
3. Which single was their first to reach No. 1 on both sides of the Atlantic?
4. Where in England did they film the video for *Island Of Lost Souls*?
5. Which British group had a No. 1 hit with their version of the 1980 chart-topper *The Tide Is High* in 2002?
6. Which single took them back to No. 1 in Britain in 1999?
7. What was the title of Debbie Harry's first solo album, released in 1981?
8. Which producer collaborated with them on the 1980 No. 1 *Call Me*?
9. Which Buddy Holly song did they cover on the album 'Parallel Lines'?
10. After they disbanded in 1982, which record label was founded by Chris Stein?

Answers

1. Richard Gottehrer
2. Nigel Harrison
3. *Heart Of Glass*
4. Tresco, Isles of Scilly
5. Atomic Kitten
6. Maria

7. 'Koo Koo'
8. Giorgio Moroder
9. *I'm Gonna Love You Too*
10. Animal

Sting and the Police

1. Who was the original Police guitarist who joined early in 1977 and left later that same year?
2. Which part did Sting play in the film version of *Quadrophenia* in 1979?
3. Which single did they issue in 1977 which was a Top 50 hit on reissue two years later?
4. The group dyed their hair blonde for a commercial filmed in February 1978 and never shown, but what was the product?
5. Where did they play the final date of their reunion tour in the US in August 2008?
6. Sting recorded *Every Breath You Take* as a duet on the album 'Without Walls' with which country singer?
7. What was the name of the jazz group he formed in February 1985?
8. Stewart Copeland released several singles and an album under what name?
9. In 1980 they issued 'Six Pack', a collection of their singles, on which coloured vinyl?
10. Which was Sting's first solo hit single, released in September 1982?

Answers

1. Henry Padovani
2. Ace Face
3. *Fall Out*
4. Wrigley's Spearmint Gum
5. Madison Square Garden

6. Tammy Wynette
7. The Blue Turtles Band
8. Klark Kent
9. Blue
10. *Spread A Little Happiness*

Dire Straits and Mark Knopfler

1. Who produced their first, eponymously-named album?
2. Which hit, with vocals by Phil Everly and Cliff Richard, also featured guitar from Mark Knopfler?
3. After seeing the group live in concert, Bob Dylan invited Knopfler and which other member of the group to play on his album 'Slow Train Coming'?
4. What was the title of their first live LP, released in 1983?
5. Who was the guest vocalist on *Money For Nothing*?
6. Which was the 14-minute long track which opened the album 'Love Over Gold'?
7. Which former Rockpile drummer joined the group in 1982?
8. Which DJ on Radio London was an early champion of the group when he played a session tape by them while they were still unsigned?
9. Which group did Mark Knopfler form to record the 1990 album 'Missing...Presumed Having a Good Time'?
10. In 2006, with whom did Knopfler collaborate on the album 'All The Roadrunning'?

Answers

1. Muff Winwood
2. *She Means Nothing To Me*
3. Pick Withers
4. 'Alchemy'
5. Sting
6. *Telegraph Road*
7. Terry Williams
8. Charlie Gillett
9. The Notting Hillbillies
10. Emmylou Harris

Elvis Costello

1. Elvis Costello's first broadcast recording was alongside his father, who wrote and sang the song, in a television commercial and won a silver award at the 1974 International Advertising Festival. What was the product?
2. Who was his manager at Stiff Records who originally suggested his change of name to Elvis Costello?
3. O the 'Live Stiffs' album, which Bacharach-David song did he perform?
4. What was the original title intended for the third album, 'Armed Forces'?
5. What was the title of his album of cover versions of country songs, recorded in Nashville in May 1981 and released that same autumn?
6. What pseudonym did he use for the release of his 1983 single, *Pills and Soap*?
7. Which band, which later became Huey Lewis and the News, provided the backing for Costello's debut album 'My Aim is True'?
8. Which organisation commissioned him to write a chamber opera based on the relationship between Hans Christian Andersen and Jenny Lind?
9. Which song, originally written and recorded by The Beatles, did he perform as a soloist at Live Aid in 1985?
10. How did the artist credit read on the UK release of his 1986 album 'King of America'?

Answers

1. R. White's Lemonade
2. Jake Riviera
3. *I Just Don't Know What To Do With Myself*
4. 'Emotional Fascism'
5. 'Almost Blue'
6. The Imposter
7. Clover
8. The Danish Royal Opera, Copenhagen. (It was never completed)
9. *All You Need Is Love*
10. The Costello Show featuring the Attractions and Confederates

Paul Weller

1. When Weller formed The Jam in 1972 playing bass guitar, who was the initial lead guitarist, who left in 1976?
2. Where did The Jam play their final concert on 11 December 1982?
3. Who played keyboards in The Style Council?
4. What was the title of the fifth and final Style Council album, which Polydor refused to release on the grounds that they did not consider it commercial enough?
5. When he formed The Paul Weller Movement in 1991, who played drums?
6. Which solo album reached No. 1 in 1995?
7. On which track on Oasis's 'What's The Story, Morning Glory' did he appear on joint lead guitar and backing vocals?
8. Which Burt Bacharach and Hal David song did he cover on the 2004 album 'Studio 150'?
9. Which Jam song did he play at the BRIT Awards in 2006 when he was presented with the Lifetime Achievement Award?
10. On which label were the albums 'Heavy Soul' and 'Heliocentric' issued?

Answers

1. Steve Brookes
2. The Brighton Centre
3. Mick Talbot
4. 'Modernism: A New Decade'
5. Steve White

6. 'Stanley Road'
7. *Champagne Supernova*
8. *Close To You*
9. *A Town Called Malice*
10. Island

Joy Division and New Order

1. Who was the vocalist with Joy Division, who died in May 1980 by his own hand?
2. What was the title of the debut Joy Division EP, recorded in December 1977 and released six months later?
3. In which studio in the Manchester area did Joy Division record their first album, 'Unknown Pleasures', in April 1978?
4. Who was the producer of Joy Division, and of New Order in their early days, and who died in 1991?
5. New Order's second album, 'Power, Corruption and Lies', released in 1983, featured a sleeve design using a still life painting of flowers from the National Gallery by which French artist?
6. With which label did New Order sign shortly after leaving Factory, and before the release of their album 'Republic' in 1993?
7. Who guested on vocals on Electronic's first single *Getting Away With It*?
8. Where did New Order play their first gig in July 1980?
9. Which veteran producer was responsible for the remix of *Blue Monday 1988*, which peaked at No.3 in the UK?
10. Who supported New Order when they played what would be their only British gig of the year, in December 1988, at the G-Mex Centre, Manchester?

Answers

1. Ian Curtis
2. 'An Ideal for Living'
3. Strawberry Studios, Stockport
4. Martin Hannett
5. Henri Fantin-Latour
6. London
7. Neil Tennant
8. Beach Club, Manchester
9. Quincy Jones
10. Happy Mondays

Depeche Mode and The Human League

1. In which town did Depeche Mode first get together in 1980?
2. Which founding member left after the first album and was thereafter part of Yazoo, The Assembly, and most notably Erasure?
3. Which was their debut single, reaching the Top 60 early in 1981?
4. In 1991, their track *Death's Door* was released on the soundtrack album for which film?
5. What was Dave Gahan's first solo album, released in 2003?
6. Before forming The Human League, Martyn Ware and Ian Craig Marsh teamed up to play together firstly as The Future and then under which other name?
7. In 1980, The Undertones had their only Top 10 single, and it included the lyrics, 'His mother bought him a synthesiser/Got the Human League in to advise her.' What was the title?
8. What was the title of their first EP, released on the Fast Product label in April 1979?
9. Jo Callis, who joined on keyboards in 1981, had previously been a member of which other group?
10. Which was their first album on EastWest records, released in 1995 after their departure from Virgin?

Answers

1. Basildon
2. Vince Clarke
3. *Dreaming Of Me*
4. *Until the End of the World*
5. 'Paper Monsters'
6. The Dead Daughters
7. *My Perfect Cousin*
8. 'The Dignity of Labour'
9. The Rezillos
10. 'Octopus'

The Pretenders

1. To which music paper in the UK did Chrissie Hynde become a contributing editor in the early 1970s, her first review being of a Neil Diamond album?
2. The group scored two major hits in the 1980s on which they were co-credited with UB40. *I Got You Babe* was the first; which was the second?
3. Who wrote their first hit, *Stop Your Sobbing*?
4. When Pete Farndon was fired from the group in 1982, who stood in on bass guitar until a permanent replacement was found?
5. *Back On The Chain Gang* became a Top 10 hit in the US in 1982 partly as a result of being used in which Robert De Niro film?
6. On which label were all their records released in the UK up to and including 1987?
7. Who joined the group on guitar in 1983 after the death of James Honeyman-Scott?
8. Which single, recorded for the soundtrack of the James Bond movie *The Living Daylights*, was released under the name Pretenders for 007?
9. Which minor hit single of 1981 by the group shared the same title as an early 1970s hit by Badfinger?
10. At which charity concert did the group perform in December 1979 alongside The Who, Wings, Elvis Costello and others at Hammersmith Odeon?

Answers

1. *New Musical Express*
2. *Breakfast In Bed*
3. Ray Davies
4. Tony Butler (of Big Country)
5. *King Of Comedy*
6. Real
7. Robbie McIntosh
8. *If There Was A Man*
9. *Day After Day*
10. Concert for Kampuchea

Iron Maiden

1. Which bass guitarist formed the group in 1975 and has been their only constant member?
2. At which pub in Maryland Point, Stratford, did an early line-up of the group have a semi-residency in 1976?
3. The group played on several dates in Britain and Europe on the 1980 Unmasked tour headlined by which American act?
4. Which song from their second album, 'Killers', was inspired by and named after a short story by Edgar Allan Poe?
5. Bruce Dickinson joined as a replacement for Paul Di'Anno in 1981 after having been vocalist with which previous group?
6. Which was the group's first Top 10 single, reaching No. 7 in 1982?
7. Which live album, a UK Top 30 success on release in 2005, had been recorded at Westfalenhalle, Dortmund, Germany, on 24 November 2003 on the Dance of Death world tour?
8. Which vocalist left Wolfsbane and replaced Bruce Dickinson in the line-up from 1994 to 1999?
9. What was the title of the Iron Maiden tribute album, issued by *Kerrang!* as a free gift in July 2008, featuring cover versions of their songs performed by Metallica, Machine Head, Dream Theater, Avenged Sevenfold and others?
10. The 2003 album 'Dance of Death' featured a track inspired by and named after which First World War battle?

Answers

1. Steve Harris
2. The Cart and Horses
3. Kiss
4. *The Murders in the Rue Morgue*
5. Samson
6. *Run to the Hills*
7. 'Death on the Road'
8. Blaze Bayley
9. 'Maiden Heaven'
10. *Passchaendaele*

The Smiths

1. Who was the group's initial bass guitarist, replaced after one gig by Andy Rourke?
2. Which was their first single to reach the UK Top 10?
3. Which of their songs, initially a B-side, caused controversy at first because the lyrics referred to the Moors murders?
4. Ivor Perry, who replaced Johnny Marr on guitar in 1987, had previously been with which other group?
5. Which was their fourth album, released in September 1987, by which time they had effectively disbanded?
6. In 1992 which reissued single gave the group their highest-ever charting 45, reaching No. 8 in the UK?
7. Which album, released in 1986, included the tracks *Frankly Mr Shankly*, *Bigmouth Strikes Again*, and *Vicar In a Tutu*?
8. Which actress appeared on the picture sleeve of their single *Ask*?
9. Which group was formed in 1988 by Johnny Marr with Bernard Sumner of New Order?
10. Which long-established but temporarily retired record label was revived by EMI for the release of Morrissey's first solo recordings in 1988?

Answers

1. Dale Hibbert
2. *Heaven Knows I'm Miserable Now*
3. *Suffer Little Children*
4. Easterhouse
5. 'Strangeways Here We Come'
6. *This Charming Man*
7. 'The Queen is Dead'
8. Yootha Joyce
9. Electronic
10. HMV (His Master's Voice)

R.E.M.

1. Which was the debut single R.E.M. released on the independent Hib-Tone label in 1981?
2. Which album, released in 1992, included the singles *Everybody Hurts* and *Nightswimming*?
3. Who produced their 1985 album 'Fables Of The Reconstruction'?
4. When all the group except Michael Stipe backed Roger McGuinn on live gigs in summer 1988, what did they call themselves?
5. With which British group did they record the album 'Athens Andover' in 1991?
6. Which track did Michael Stipe contribute to the Walt Disney compilation 'Stay Awake' in 1988?
7. Which was the first album they recorded for and released on Warner Bros in 1988?
8. Under what name did they play two sets at the Borderline Club, London, in March 1991?
9. Which singer from the B52's sang guest vocals on the 1991 hit *Shiny Happy People*?
10. Which song did they contribute to the Leonard Cohen tribute collection, 'I'm Your Fan', released in 1991?

Answers

1. *Radio Free Europe*
2. 'Automatic For The People'
3. Joe Boyd
4. Southern Gentlemen
5. The Troggs

6. *Little April Shower*
7. 'Green'
8. Bingo Hand Job
9. Kate Pierson
10. *First We Take Manhattan*

Prince

1. What is Prince's full name in real life?
2. Which was his first US single, released in June 1978?
3. For which vocalist was he the opening act on the 1980 Fire It Up tour?
4. Which was his first UK Top 10 single, reaching No. 4, and also his first US No. 1, both in 1984?
5, Which of his songs was subsequently covered by Tom Jones and the Art of Noise, becoming a UK Top 10 hit in 1988?
6. Released in 1985, which of his albums included the singles *Raspberry Beret* and *Pop Life*?
7. With which British singer did he duet in 1987 on *U Got the Look*?
8. In 1994, which single became his only UK No. 1?
9. With which singer did he perform at the opening of the Grammy Awards in February 2004?
10. On which Stevie Wonder single, recorded in 2005, did he play guitar, while En Vogue were featured on backing vocals?

Answers

1. Prince Rogers Nelson
2. *Soft And Wet*
3. Rick James
4. *When Doves Cry*

5. *Kiss*
6. 'Around The World In a Day'
7. Sheena Easton
8. *The Most Beautiful Girl In The World*
9. Beyonce Knowles
10. *So What The Fuss*

George Michael

1. On which record label were the original Wham! hits released in 1982 and 1983?
2. Which female film star's name completes the line 'You make the sun shine brighter than Doris Day', from *Wake Me Up Before You Go-Go*?
3. Wham! became the first Western group to tour which country in April 1985?
4. Which musician and songwriter, who had previously had two Top 10 hits as a solo performer, produced the No. 1 duet with Aretha Franklin *I Knew You Were Waiting For Me*?
5. Which song did he perform with Queen at the Freddie Mercury Tribute Concert at Wembley Stadium in April 1992, becoming the lead track on the No. 1 'Five Live' EP one year later?
6. To which charity did he donate the royalties for his 1996 No. 1, *Jesus to a Child*?
7. Which song, a Top 10 hit in 2000, was recorded by Whitney Houston two years earlier and was credited as a duet with George after his vocals were added?
8. Which was his first album released with Sony in 2004 after he re-signed with them, following his departure in 1995 after a legal dispute?
9. Which single, a 2002 Top 10 hit, included samples from The Human League's *Love Action* and ABC's *Be Near Me*?
10. On which TV quiz programme did he appear in 2003 with Ronan Keating. raising £32,000 between them for charity?

Answers

1. Innervision
2. Doris Day
3. China
4. Narada Michael Walden
5. *Somebody to Love*
6. Childline
7. *If I Told You That*
8. 'Patience'
9. *Freeek!*
10. *Who Wants To Be a Millionaire?*

The Pet Shop Boys

1. Of which magazine was Neil Tennant the assistant editor when he first met Chris Lowe?
2. To which label did they sign briefly, and which released their first version of *West End Girls* in 1984?
3. Which female singer performed part of the vocals on *What Have I Done To Deserve This*?
4. What was the title of their first album, released in 1986?
5. With whom did they collaborate on writing the West End musical *Closer To Heaven*, which opened in May 2001?
6. On which Top 10 hit in 1989 did they collaborate with Liza Minnelli?
7. What was the title of the compilation of their 2-CD compilation of B-sides, released in 1995?
8. Who had the original hit version in 1979 of *Go West*, which became a No. 2 hit for them in 1993?
9. Where in London did they play at a fund-raising gala for the Red Hot Aids Charitable Trust to celebrate the release of 'Twentieth Century Blues – The Songs Of Noel Coward', in January 1998?
10. With which singer did they perform at the BRIT Awards in 1996?

Answers

1. *Smash Hits*
2. Epic

3. Dusty Springfield
4. 'Please'
5. Jonathan Harvey
6. *Losing My Mind*
7. 'Alternative'
8. Village People
9. Park Lane Hotel
10. David Bowie

Take That

1. Which was the group's first Top 40 single, reaching No. 38 in 1991?
2. Who was the bassist with the Edgar Winter Group who later had hits as a soloist, and wrote and recorded the original version of *Relight My Fire*, a No. 1 for the group and Lulu in 1993?
3. On which TV show did the group make their debut in 1990, singing the as-yet unreleased song *My Kind Of Girl*?
4. On which label were all their records issued between 1991 and 1996?
5. In which city, in mainland Europe, did they give their final performance in April 1996 before disbanding?
6. Which was their first single to be released after they reformed in 2006?
7. Which member's departure from the group was announced in September 2014?
8. What was the title of Mark Owen's first solo album, released in 1996?
9. Who was Robbie Williams' songwriting partner and co-writer of several of his hits, including *Angels* and *Let Me Entertain You*?
10. How many singles were released in Britain from the album 'Everything Changes'?

Answers

1. *Promises*
2. *Relight My Fire*
3. *The Hit Man And Her*

4. RCA
5. Amsterdam
6. *Patience*
7. Jason Orange
8. 'Green Man'
9. Guy Chambers
10. 6

Ed Sheeran

1. To which major record label, initially known in the early 1970s as the home of major American acts, did he sign in January 2011?
2. Which was his debut hit single, entering the chart at No. 3 in June 2011?
3. Which group did he support on their US tour from March to May 2012?
4. For which charity did he perform a gig on 24 March 2014 at the Royal Albert Hall, London, where he where he played Take It Back' for the first time?
5. Which of his albums included the singles *Sing*, *Don't*, and *Thinking Out Loud*?
6. What was the name of his record label which he launched in 2015 and to which Jamie Lawson was the first artist he signed?
7. Which guitarist did he join on stage at the Nippon Budokan, Tokyo, on 13 April 2016, on the song *I Will Be There*, as well as playing guitar himself on the same song on that guitarist's subsequent album 'I Still Do'?
8. From which university did he receive an honorary degree in October 2015 for his 'outstanding contribution to music'?
9. Which of his songs became the most streamed song on Spotify on 21 September 2017 with over 1.32 billion streams, and the best-selling UK single that year?
10. *Perfect Duet*, the Christmas No. 1 in 2017, was a duet with which female singer?

Answers

1. Asylum
2. *The A Team*
3. Snow Patrol
4. Teenage Cancer Trust
5. 'X' (or Multiply)
6. Gingerbread Man
7. Eric Clapton
8. University of Suffolk, Ipswich
9. *Shape of You*
10. Beyoncé

John Peel

A few questions about the man who was arguably the most influential DJ in British broadcasting history.

1. Which American blues-rock group did Peel champion while working as a DJ in the US and bring to England in 1966, resulting in the release of their single *I Can Take You to the Sun*?
2. For which radio station in the mid-1960s did he present a show called *The Perfumed Garden*?
3. Which show did he present on Radio 1 from October 1967, initially with Pete Drummond and various other DJs, then on his own?
4. What name did his family give to the dance which he described as his own personalised boogie, 'a kind of energetic, springy, shuffling walk on the spot'?
5. Which performer played a session for Peel's Christmas Day 1973 show as a pub pianist, allegedly 'destroying' or sending up some of his own hits?
6. On which BBC TV comedy programme in 1973 did he appear on one episode as a compere on *Top Of The Pops*, wearing a blonde wig?
7. Which track was voted No. 1 in the first Peel's Festive 50, broadcast at the end of 1976?
8. Which fellow Radio 1 DJ did Peel refer to as his 'rhythm pal' and sometimes co-present *Top of the Pops* with in the early 1980s?
9. For which Radio 1 daytime presenter did he stand in for one week on the lunchtime weekday show in April 1993?
10. To which country had he and his wife gone on holiday when he suddenly died in October 2004?

Answers

1. The Misunderstood
2. Radio London
3. Top Gear
4. The Westbourne Grove Walk
5. Elton John
6. *The Goodies*
7. *Stairway to Heaven*, Led Zeppelin
8. David ('Kid') Jensen
9. Jakki Brambles
10. Peru

Who's for cards?

All the answers in this round are associated with playing cards, though in one or two cases a little tenuously.

1. A single which had originally been an American No. 1 in 1974, and after being reissued in Britain several times, reached No. 1 in 1990 after being used in a TV advert for jeans.
2. A Top 20 hit in 1980 and the title track of an album by Motörhead.
3. The first British hit for KC and the Sunshine Band.
4. A nine-minute epic by Bob Dylan from 'Blood on the Tracks'.
5. A song by Hank DeVito which was a hit in Britain in 1979 for Dave Edmunds and in America two years later for Juice Newton.
6. A record released by Ned Miller in 1957 which failed to chart until reissued five years later.
7. A 'death disc' by the Boomtown Rats in 1979.
8. Another 'death disc' by the Shangri-Las, which became a British hit in 1965, 1972 and again in 1976.
9. The title track of the debut album by Sade.
10. A traditional gambling song, thought to originate from Texas and made popular by Blind Lemon Jefferson. A 1960s version, credited to Bob Dylan and Ben Carruthers, was covered on the first Fairport Convention album.

Answers

1. *The Joker*
2. *Ace of Spades*
3. *Queen of Clubs*
4. *Lily, Rosemary and the Jack of Hearts*
5. *Queen of Hearts*
6. *From a Jack to a King*
7. *Diamond Smiles*
8. *Leader of the Pack*
9. *Diamond Life*
10. *Jack of Diamonds*

A little classical gas

The answers to the following are hit songs partly inspired by pieces of classical music.

1. A hit for the Beach Boys in 1979, their first British hit for nine years, based partly on Bach's *Jesu, Joy of Man's Desiring*.
2. A song co-written by Barry Manilow and Adrienne Anderson, which became a hit in the 1970s for Barry, for Donna Summer, and in the 1990s for Take That, based on Chopin's *Prelude in C Minor*, Opus 28, No 20.
3. A hit for The Move in 1967, with a guitar riff based on a movement of Tchaikovsky's *1812 Overture*.
4. A hit for the Piltdown Men in 1961, adapted from Rossini's *William Tell Overture*.
5. A hit for Manfred Mann's Earth Band in 1973, interpolating a short section from *Jupiter*, from Holst's *The Planets*.
6. A hit for Love Sculpture in 1968, basically a rock arrangement of a piece by Khachaturian.
7. A hit for the Toys in 1965, based on Bach's *Minuet in G*.
8. A Christmas novelty hit for George Cole and Dennis Waterman in 1983, interpolating part of Holst's *In the Bleak Midwinter*.
9. A hit for Eric Carmen in 1986, incorporating a short section from Rachmaninov's *Symphony No. 2*.
10. A hit for the Cougars in 1963, based on a movement from Tchaikovsky's *Swan Lake*.

Answers

1. *Lady Lynda*
2. *Could It Be Magic*
3. *Night Of Fear*
4. *Piltdown Rides Again*
5. *Joybringer*
6. *Sabre Dance*
7. *A Lover's Concerto*
8. *What Are We Gonna Get 'Er Indoors*
9. *All By Myself*
10. *Saturday Nite At The Duckpond*

Let's go to London

Can you identify the artists most associated with the following?

1. *Streets of London*
2. *Last Train to London*
3. *London Calling*
4. *(I Don't Want To Go To) Chelsea*
5. 'Solo in Soho' – a 1980 solo album from the front man of a successful group
6. *London Boys*
7. *Euston Station*
8. *London Lady*
9. *Waterloo Sunset*
10. *Baker Street*

Answers

1. Ralph McTell
2. ELO
3. The Clash
4. Elvis Costello and the Attractions
5. Phil Lynott
6. T. Rex
7. Barbara Ruskin
8. The Stranglers
9. The Kinks
10. Gerry Rafferty

Let's go to the movies

Can you identify the following films from the clues?

1. The Beatles, accompanied by Paul's uncle, take a train to London where they are to appear on a television programme. Also includes Wilfred Brambell and Victor Spinetti (1964)
2. Gangster Fats Murdoch wants to make his fiancée Georgy into a star, but it goes wrong when the agent he hires to promote her falls in love with and marries her. Stars Edmund O'Brien and Jayne Mansfield, with a soundtrack including Little Richard, Eddie Cochran and Gene Vincent (1956)
3. Two bikers, Billy and Wyatt, celebrate the conclusion of a coke deal by going to a Mardi Gras festival at New Orleans. Stars Dennis Hopper and Peter Fonda, with a soundtrack including Steppenwolf and the Byrds (1969)
4. A documentary based around Bob Dylan's two-week British tour, from concert hall and hotel room to his travels by car and train. Also includes Albert Grossman, Joan Baez, Donovan and Alan Price (1965)
5. A punk fantasy with Queen Elizabeth I coming to life in the punk era. Stars Toyah Wilcox, Jordan and Adam Ant (1978)
6. A deaf, dumb and blind boy becomes a pinball champion. Stars Roger Daltrey, Ann-Margret, Oliver Reed and Robert Powell (1975)
7. Tony Manero works as a paint store clerk in Brooklyn, New York, but really lives for the

weekends when he and his friends can strut their stuff on the dance floor. Stars John Travolta and Karen Lynn Gorney, with a soundtrack including the Bee Gees (1977)
8. The Sex Pistols tell their own story in a documentary directed by Julien Temple (2000)
9. A newly-wed couple's car breaks down in bad weather and they seek shelter at the house of transvestite Dr Frank'n'Furter. Stars Tim Curry, Little Nell, and Richard O'Brien (1975)
10. A collage of film clips and surrealistic sketches showing a day in the life of the Monkees. Also includes Annette Funicello and Jack Nicholson (1968)

Answers

1. *A Hard Day's Night*
2. *The Girl Can't Help It*
3. *Easy Rider*
4. *Don't Look Back*
5. *Jubilee*
6. *Tommy*
7. *Saturday Night Fever*
8. *The Filth And The Fury*
9. *The Rocky Horror Picture Show*
10. *Head*

They wrote books too

Singers and musicians have also written and published books of memoirs, poetry and occasionally fiction as well. Can you name the authors of the following?

1. *Tarantula*
2. *Is That It?*
3. *The Warlock of Love*
4. *Ode to a High Flying Bird*
5. *Diary of a Rock and Roll Star*
6. *The Final Run*
7. *I Me Mine*
8. *Been Down So Long It Looks Like Up To Me*
9. *The Lords and the New Creatures*
10. *In His Own Write*

Answers

1. Bob Dylan
2. Bob Geldof
3. Marc Bolan
4. Charlie Watts
5. Ian Hunter
6. Tommy Steele
7. George Harrison
8. Richard Farina
9. Jim Morrison
10. John Lennon

The name's the same

It would hardly be surprising if there were not occasional cases of performers or groups sharing the same name – sometimes years apart. Can you guess the following?

1. The British psych-pop duo of the 1960s best remembered for their Top 40 hit *Rainbow Chaser*, and a popular American grunge rock group of the early 1990s whose success was cut short after their front man took his own life in 1994.
2. The 1980s hitmaker best remembered for *Wherever I Lay My Hat*, and the vocalist formerly with Sad Café and later Mike of the Mechanics.
3. The Irish group formed in 1967 that briefly featured future Thin Lizzy members Phil Lynott and Gary Moore, and the American group whose most successful hit was *18 and Life* in 1989.
4. The trumpeter and bandleader who fronted The Button Down Brass, and the front man of one of the most enduring British groups who had three chart-topping singles in the 1960s whose services to music were recognised by a knighthood for services to the arts in 2017.
5. The British group formed in the late 1960s by brothers Paul and Adrian Gurvitz who had a Top 10 hit in 1968 with *Race with the Devil*, and the Scottish group whose cover version of Cameo's *Word Up* made the Top 10 in 1994.
6. The bass guitarist who played successively with The Move and Wizzard in the late 1960s and early 1970s, and another player of the same instrument with The Georgia Satellites in the 1980s.

7. The much-loved comedy duo who had a posthumous No. 2 hit around Christmas 1975 taken from the soundtrack of a 1937 film, and a British reggae cockney duo of the 1980s who had a minor hit with *Clunk Click*.
8. The very successful American rock group who peaked in the mid-1970s and reformed in 1994 after an acrimonious split in 1980, the American R'n'B group who released three singles there in 1954, the British group from Bristol who released several singles in the early 1960s, and the Jamaican group whose career spanned the later 1960s and early 1970s.
9. The guitarist, banjo and jug player from Mungo Jerry' early days, and the front man of a successful mid-1980s British group who took their name from his surname, who later had a minor solo hit.
10. The British songwriter who collaborated with Doug Flett on several pop hits from the late 1960s onwards for Cliff Richard, The Hollies and others, and the keyboard player with Dire Straits - who is his nephew.

Answers

1. Nirvana
2. Paul Young
3. Skid Row
4. Ray Davies
5. Cameo
6. Rick Price
7. Laurel and Hardy
8. The Eagles
9. Paul King
10. Guy Fletcher

It's still rock'n'roll to me

1. Who scored the first of three American No. 1 hits, and his first British Top 20 success, in 1980 with the above title?
2. When John McEnroe, Pat Cash and The Full Metal Rackets recorded their version of Led Zeppelin's *Rock and Roll* as a charity single in 1991, who provided the lead vocal?
3. What was the full title (including words in brackets) of Kevin Johnson's only Top 30 hit in 1975?
4. Which Chuck Berry song was covered by The Beatles on their fourth album 'Beatles For Sale', with George Martin on piano?
5. Whose British chart debut in 1977 was *Anything That's Rock'n'Roll*?
6. Whose ballad *Rock'n'Roll* appeared on their 1980 Top 10 album 'Just Supposin'' and became a Top 10 single, in edited form, just over a year later?
7. Who had a Top 10 single and album in 1974 with 'It's Only Rock'n'Roll (But I Like It)'?
8. Which rather morbid David Bowie title, originally an album track from 'The Rise And Fall of Ziggy Stardust and The Spiders From Mars', gave him a Top 30 hit in 1974?
9. *I Love Rock'n'Roll* was a major transatlantic hit for Joan Jett and The Blackhearts in 1982, but which group originally recorded and released it as a single in 1975?
10. Who claimed *Rock'n'Roll is King* in 1983 in what was to be their final British Top 20 hit?

Answers

1. Billy Joel
2. Roger Daltrey
3. *Rock'n'Roll (I Gave You The Best Years Of My Life)*
4. *Rock'n'Roll Music*
5. Tom Petty & the Heartbreakers
6. Status Quo
7. Rolling Stones
8. *Rock and Roll Suicide*
9. The Arrows
10. ELO

How sweet they are

1. Which song gave brother and sister duo Mac and Katie Kissoon a top three hit in 1975?
2. Which song was a No. 1 for New Edition in 1983?
3. Which single by Strawberry Alarm Clock topped the US chart for one week in November 1967 although it failed in the UK?
4. Which Australian group had their only UK hit, a Top 10 success, in 1976 with *Howzat*?
5. Which song gave the Archies a transatlantic No.1 in 1969?
6. Which song, a No. 1 in 1998, came from the animated TV show *South Park*, was credited to Chef, and featured the vocals of Isaac Hayes?
7. What invitation did Def Leppard send out in 1987, on their second single from the album 'Hysteria'?
8. Which track from the Beatles' White Album was written by George Harrison and inspired by Eric Clapton's love of chocolate?
9. Which title was shared by a 1976 hit for Sheer Elegance and also a song recorded by Syd Barrett as a soloist in 1970, appearing on his outtakes album 'Opel' in 1988?
10. Which country song, which was really about flowers but could have referred to a well-known box or tin of chocolates, was a hit in the US for George Jones in 1970 and Elvis Costello in 1981?

Answers

1. *Sugar Candy Kisses*
2. *Candy Girl*
3. *Incense and Peppermints*
4. Sherbet
5. *Sugar Sugar*
6. *Chocolate Salty Balls*
7. *Pour Some Sugar On Me*
8. *Savoy Truffle*
9. *Milky Way*
10. *Good Year For The Roses*

The 50s

1. *Rock Around The Clock* was featured over the opening credits of which movie?
2. Which was the first group to have a UK No. 1 single after the charts were launched in November 1952?
3. Cliff Richard's first hit *Move It* had originally been the B-side of the single. What was on the A-side?
4. In which year was Sun Records founded by Sam Phillips?
5. Whose real name was Vincent Eugene Craddock?
6. Which female artist had five simultaneous hits in the Top 20 of the chart on 17 March 1955?
7. Which song was a hit in 1958 on separate versions by Alma Cogan and the McGuire Sisters?
8. Frankie Laine's *I Believe* had three separate runs at No. 1 in 1953. For how many weeks altogether was it at the top?
9. Which Buddy Holly single gave him his only No. 1 shortly after his death in 1959?
10. Members of the Primes and Otis Williams later joined to form which Motown group?
11. In which city was Eddie Cochran born?
12. By what name was Concetta Franconero better known?
13. On which record label were the first Elvis Presley hits in the UK released, before they appeared on RCA?

14. In 1954 Rosemary Clooney and Billie Anthony both had hits with which song which would also be No. 1 in 1981?
15. Although best remembered as a TV presenter, who had a hit in 1956 with *The Shifting Whispering Sands*?
16. When the album chart was launched in 1958, the first No. 1 was a soundtrack, and stayed there 70 weeks – which?
17. Which Jerome Kern song from the 1933 musical *Roberta* was a No. 1 for the Platters in 1959?
18. He was married to Debbie Reynolds when he topped the UK chart in 1953, and their daughter Carrie later married Paul Simon – who was he?
19. Which jazz singer, who died in 1959, was sometimes known as Lady Day?
20. Which comedy film actor had a Top 10 hit in 1954 with *Don't Laugh At Me*?
21. Which record was in the Top 10 at Christmas 1957, and was reissued to top the Christmas chart in 1986?
22. In which year did Chuck Berry have a Top 20 hit with *Sweet Little Sixteen*?
23. Whose hits included *The Little Shoemaker, Majorca* and *With All My Heart*?
24. Little Richard had a hit in 1957 with a song from, and with the same name as, a film starring Jayne Mansfield; what was the title?
25 Who was the only instrumental artist to have consecutive UK No. 1's in the decade?
26. Which song gave Andy Williams a No. 1, his only chart-topper ever, in 1957?
27. Which country singer died on 1 January 1953?
28. *Memories Are Made Of This* was the only transatlantic No. 1 in the 1950s for whom?

29. What nickname was given to Eddie Calvert, who had a No. 1 with *O Mein Papa?*
30. Which songwriting partnership wrote the Coasters' *Yakety Yak, Along Came Jones*, and several early hits by Elvis Presley?
31. Craig Douglas and Sam Cooke were competing in the 1959 charts with their own versions of which song?
32. The rivalry between the Jets and the Sharks, two New York City street gangs, is the basis for the story of which musical?
33. Tom and Jerry made their first single *Hey Schoolgirl* in 1957, but under what name did they later become famous?
34. Which disc jockey styled himself King of the Moondogs?
35. Which singer was known as 'the King of Calypso' after the success of his 1956 album *Calypso*?
36. In which year did RCA Records issue the first stereo LPs?
37. A song about which battle gave Johnny Horton a US No. 1 in 1959?
38. Which song topped the charts in separate versions by Guy Mitchell and Tommy Steele, and gave Dave Edmunds and Cliff Richard respectively minor hit versions some years later?
39. Which song written by Merle Travis in 1947 became a No. 1 for Tennessee Ernie Ford in 1956?
40. From which musical work did Bobby Darin's *Mack The Knife* come?
41. The Farina Brothers had a hit in 1959 with *Sleepwalk*, but how were they better known?
42. *What Do You Want*, by Adam Faith, was the first UK No. 1 for which record label?

43. Ross Bagdasarian, alias David Seville, created which novelty group?
44. Which song was co-written by a future American Vice-President in 1912, topped the charts on both sides of the Atlantic in 1958, and was later a UK hit for Cliff Richard and later still the Four Tops?
45. Born in Trinidad, who became the first black artist to top the UK charts, and the only female instrumentalist who ever achieved this feat?
46. In the UK and US, what was the first song with the words rock and roll in the title to reach No. 1?
47. Who topped the UK charts twice in the 1950s, and had his final top three hit in 1971 with a song written by Don McLean?
48. Which Sam Cooke song gave Craig Douglas a No. 1 in 1959?
49. Banjo player and vocalist with the Chris Barber band and later a solo hit artist, who was the 'King of Skiffle'?
50. Which two aspiring teenage guitarists and singers first met at St Peter's Church fete, Liverpool, on 6 July 1957?

Answers

1. *Blackboard Jungle*?
2. The Stargazers
3. *Schoolboy Crush*
4. 1952
5. Gene Vincent
6. Ruby Murray
7. *Sugartime*
8. 18
9. *It Doesn't Matter Anymore*

10. The Temptations
11. Oklahoma
12. Connie Francis
13. His Master's Voice (HMV)
14. *This Ole House*
15. Eamonn Andrews
16. *South Pacific*
17. *Smoke Gets In Your Eyes*
18. Eddie Fisher
19. Billie Holliday
20. Norman Wisdom
21. *Reet Petite*, Jackie Wilson
22. 1958
23. Petula Clark
24. *The Girl Can't Help It*
25. Russ Conway
26. *Butterfly*
27. Hank Williams
28. Dean Martin
29. The man with the golden trumpet
30. Jerry Leiber and Mike Stoller
31. *Only Sixteen*
32. *West Side Story*
33. Simon and Garfunkel
34. Alan Freed
35. Harry Belafonte
36. 1958
37. New Orleans
38. *Singing The Blues*
39. *Sixteen Tons*
40. *Threepenny Opera*
41. Santo and Johnny
42. Parlophone
43. The Chipmunks
44. *It's All In the Game*
45. Winifred Atwell
46. *Rock'n'Roll Waltz,* Kay Starr

47. Perry Como
48. *Only Sixteen*
49. Lonnie Donegan
50. John Lennon and Paul McCartney (who, er, went on to form a group called The Beatles)

The 60s – Part 1

1. Whose debut hit was *Sweets For My Sweet*?
2. Which group included Paul McCartney's younger brother Mike?
3. Which month had a bad weather connection for hits by Dinah Washington and Carole King?
4. In which group were Dean Ford (real name Thomas McAleese) and Junior Campbell the songwriters?
5. Which No. 1 in 1964 was reissued to make No. 25 in 1972 and No. 11 in 1982?
6. Which comedian had a Top 40 hit in 1969 with *If You Love Her*?
7. Which song was a US Top five hit for Gene McDaniels and a UK No. 1 for Frankie Vaughan in 1961?
8. Which female vocalist had two consecutive chart-toppers in 1964?
9. Which No. 1 was partly inspired by Bach's *Air On A G String?*
10. Which group were sued for libel by Harold Wilson when they promoted their third single with a scurrilous postcard, and had to give all the record's royalties to charity?
11. Who played lead guitar on Joe Cocker's *With A Little Help From My Friends?*
12. What was the Supremes' first US No. 1?
13. Which record producer shot his landlady and himself dead on 3 February 1967?
14. In 1960 *Happy Go Lucky Me* was the only Top 40 hit for which popular 1940s film star?

15. Where was the festival of 1967 held which included The Jimi Hendrix Experience, The Byrds, The Who and Otis Redding?
16. Which 1964 chart-topping group had a female drummer?
17. At which venue did Cream play their farewell gig in November 1968?
18. By what name was Charles Weedon Westover better known?
19. Which member of Traffic wrote their No 2 hit *Hole In My Shoe*?
20. In which Essex town were Brian Poole and the Tremeloes based?
21. Bernie Calvert replaced Eric Haydock on bass guitar in which group?
22. *Bird On The Wire* was the opening track on which Leonard Cohen album?
23. *Debora* was one of only two Tyrannosaurus Rex singles to reach the Top 30. Which was the other?
24. Roy Orbison had three No. 1 singles in the UK. Which was the first?
25. 'Massachusetts', a No. 1 hit for the Bee Gees, was originally written for which other group to record?
26. Ronald Wycherley had several hits, but under what name?
27. The first three singles by which British group all reached No. 1, in 1963?
28. Who was the vocalist, guitarist, and main songwriter in the Idle Race?
29. *Tell Me When* was the first record by a Birmingham group to make the Top 10, but which was the group?
30. Which instrumental hit spent over a year in the Top 50, in 1961-62?

31. Which movie soundtrack album spent 70 non-consecutive weeks at No. 1 between 1965 and 1968?
32. On the sleeve of the album 'John Mayall's Bluesbreakers', what is Eric Clapton seen reading?
33. Which comedian had his most successful single in 1965 with *Tears*?
34. With which group did Christine Perfect, later Christine McVie, have chart success in the late 1960s before joining Fleetwood Mac?
35. Which album track from 1968, released as a single and making the Top 30 four years later, begins 'Let us be lovers, we'll marry our fortunes together'?
36. *Hang On Sloopy* by the McCoys was the first hit on which label?
37. Who was replaced as vocalist in Deep Purple by Ian Gillan in 1969?
38. In 1968 Cupid's Inspiration had the only Top 10 hit on the NEMS label – what was it?
39. Which song from the 1942 movie *The Fleet's Inn* was recorded and became a No. 1 hit in 1962?
40. Clem Cattini was one of the most in-demand session musicians of the 60s and 70s, on which instrument?
41. In which year was the first Isle of Wight Festival?
42. Which cathedral did the New Vaudeville Band sing about in 1966?
43. Who recorded the original version of *My White Bicycle* in 1967, a hit for Nazareth eight years later?
44. What was Matt Monro's real name?
45. Alan Taylor, Johnny Tebb, Howard Newcombe and Robert O'Brian were members

of which group whose most successful record reached No. 2 in 1968?
46. On whose farm was the Woodstock Festival held in 1969?
47. *The Dock Of The Bay* by Otis Redding and *In The Midnight Hour* by Wilson Pickett were co-written by each singer with which guitarist?
48. Who sang backing vocals on Fontella Bass's *Rescue Me*, and had a No. 2 hit as a soloist in 1975, but died of cancer four years later?
49. What was Adam Faith's final UK Top 50 hit, in 1966?
50. Before Marvin Gaye, who had the original, less successful hit version of *I Heard It Through The Grapevine?*

Answers

1. The Searchers
2. The Scaffold
3. September
4. Marmalade
5. *The House Of the Rising Sun,* Animals
6. Dick Emery
7. *Tower Of Strength*
8. Cilla Black
9. *A Whiter Shade Of Pale,* Procol Harum
10. The Move
11. Jimmy Page
12. *Where Did Our Love Go?*
13. Joe Meek
14. George Formby
15. Monterey, California
16. The Honeycombs
17. Royal Albert Hall
18. Del Shannon

19. Dave Mason
20. Dagenham
21. The Hollies
22. 'Songs From A Room'
23. *One Inch Rock*
24. *Only The Lonely*
25. The Seekers
26. Billy Fury
27. Gerry and the Pacemakers
28. Jeff Lynne
29. The Applejacks
30. *Stranger On The Shore*, by Acker Bilk
31. 'The Sound Of Music'
32. The Beano
33. Ken Dodd
34. Chicken Shack
35. *America*, by Simon & Garfunkel
36. Immediate
37. Rod Evans
38. *Yesterday Has Gone*
39. *I Remember You*
40. Drums
41. 1968
42. Winchester
43. Tomorrow
44. Terry Parsons
45. The Casuals
46. Max Yasgur
47. Steve Cropper
48. Minnie Riperton
49. *Cheryl's Going Home*
50. Gladys Knight and the Pips

The 60s – Part 2

1. Until they launched Apple Records, on which label were all The Beatles' records released in the UK?
2. Which group did Ian Gillan and Roger Glover leave towards the end of the decade for Deep Purple?
3. Who was the vocalist with Tomorrow, but better remembered for the hit *Excerpt From A Teenage Opera*?
4. Which Irish group had more success with albums than singles, yet still had hits with *Seven Drunken Nights and Black Velvet Band*?
5. Which group was fronted by Bob Hite, sometimes nicknamed ''the bear'?
6. Which was the only No. 1 single for Jim Reeves?
7. Which comedy star, later renowned ornithologist, released a single in 1969 called *Jimmy Young*?
8. Which was the most successful single by Them?
9. In 1963, The Beatles' *She Loves You* was No. 1 for four weeks, then returned to the top after an interval of seven weeks. Name either of the two records to reach No. 1 during that interval.
10. Which album by Duke Ellington spent two weeks in the album chart in 1961?
11. Only two American acts topped the British singles chart in 1964; The Supremes, and which solo artist?

12. What was the B-side of Jeff Beck's 1968 single *Love is Blue*, which became a Top 30 hit in 1973?
13. Which group's only chart album, in 1967, was 'Without Reservations'?
14. Which Bob Dylan song gave The Jimi Hendrix Experience a Top 10 hit in 1968?
15. *Handbags and Gladrags* was recorded by several artists during the decade, but who was the only performer to make it a Top 40 hit?
16. *Build Me Up Buttercup*, a hit for The Foundations, had originally been intended for which all-girl group to record?
17. Mike Sarne's 1962 UK No. 1 *Come Outside* featured call-and-respond spoken vocals from which future sitcom and soap opera actress?
18. Nilsson's first hit single, *Everybody's Talkin'*, was taken from which movie?
19. Which songwriting partnership was responsible for all the hits by Dave Dee, Dozy, Beaky, Mick and Tich, and The Herd?
20. Which successful group began as Dean Ford and the Gaylords?
21. Which song gave both the Temptations and Otis Redding their first UK hit?
22. *Homburg* was the second (and in fact last) Top 10 hit for which group?
23. Which was Chuck Berry's only UK top three single of the decade?
24. Before he helped to found Cream, of which chart-topping group was bass guitarist Jack Bruce briefly a member?
25. On which Rolling Stones hit did John Lennon and Paul McCartney contribute to backing vocals?

26. Who had Top 10 albums in 1966 with 'Going Places' and 'Whipped Cream and Other Delights'?
27. Who was 'Bobby's girl' in 1962?
28. In which year was Bill Haley and his Comets' *Rock Around the Clock* reissued and back in the Top 20?
29. What was Lonnie Donegan's Christmas Top 30 hit of 1960?
30. Who narrowly missed No. 1 in 1961 and 1962 with *Lazy River* and *Thing*s?
31. Which song, written by Roy Wood, became in 1969 the only single ever released by Acid Gallery?
32. Which Wolverhampton group released their first album 'Beginnings' in 1969, but found much greater success in the 1970s after shortening their name?
33. Which pairing of soloist and group had their only hit with *Goo Goo Barabajagal (Love is Hot)*?
34. Which group had their only hit with a cover version of The Beatles' *I Should Have Known Better*?
35. Although better remembered as a producer, Mickie Most had a minor Top 50 hit in 1963 with which single?
36. For which singer was a cover version of Sam Cooke's *Cupid* a hit in 1969?
37. In 1968, which was the first group to top the album chart with a compilation of their greatest hits?
38. Although less well-remembered as a singer, who had hits in 1968 and 1969 with *So Much Love* and *It's Only Love*?
39. Which instrument did Al Kooper play on Bob Dylan's *Like a Rolling Stone*?

40. Which group's most successful singles were *She'd Rather Be With Me* and *Elenore*?
41. Future producer Mike Hurst was a guitarist in which folk-pop trio, which also included a brother and sister?
42. The Beatles had the Christmas No. 1 in 1963, 1964, 1965 and 1967. Which group or performer did so in 1966, and with which record?
43. Derek Leckenby was the lead guitarist of which group?
44. Which was the only hit single ever, a Top 10 record in 1968, on the Marmalade label?
45. Which record gave Ricky Valance a No. 1 in 1960 in spite of (or perhaps because of) being banned by the BBC, because it was about death in a stock car race?
46. Which chart-topper from 1966 was sampled by Ash on their 2001 hit *Candy*?
47. Which was the Troggs' home town?
48. Which trio comprised Con and Declan Cluskey, and Sean Stokes?
49. Although the Love Affair took it to No. 1, who had previously recorded *Everlasting Love* and still had a minor hit with it at the same time?
50. Which was the only hit for the Kasenetz-Katz Singing Orchestral Circus?

Answers

1. Parlophone
2. Episode Six
3. Keith West
4. The Dubliners
5. Canned Heat
6. *Distant Drums*

7. Bill Oddie
8. *Here Comes the Night*
9. *Do You Love Me*, Brian Poole and the Tremeloes; *You'll Never Walk Alone*, Gerry and the Pacemakers
10. 'Nut Cracker Suite'
11. Roy Orbison
12. *I've Been Drinking*
13. Simon Dupree and the Big Sound
14. *All Along the Watchtower*
15. Chris Farlowe
16. The Paper Dolls
17. Wendy Richard
18. Midnight Cowboy
19. Howard Blaikley (Ken Howard and Alan Blaikley)
20. Marmalade
21. *My Girl*
22. Procol Harum
23. *No Particular Place To Go*
24. Manfred Mann
25. *We Love You*
26. Herb Alpert and his Tijuana Brass
27. Susan Maughan
28. 1968
29. Virgin Mary
30. Bobby Darin
31. *Dance Round the Maypole*
32. Ambrose Slade
33. Donovan and the Jeff Beck Group
34. The Naturals
35. *Mister Porter*
36. Johnny Nash
37. The Four Tops
38. Tony Blackburn
39. Organ
40. The Turtles

41. The Springfields
42. Tom Jones, *The Green Green Grass of Home*
43. Herman's Hermits
44. *This Wheel's on Fire*, Julie Driscoll, Brian Auger, and the Trinity
45. *Tell Laura I Love Her*
46. *Make It Easy On Yourself*, The Walker Brothers
47. Andover
48. The Bachelors
49. Robert Knight
50. *Quick Joey Small (Run Joey Run)*

The 70s – Part 1

1. Who topped the album chart with *Night Flight to Venus* and *Oceans of Fantasy?*
2. Who was nicknamed The Walrus of Love (or Lurve)?
3. When Bob Dylan briefly left CBS in 1973, he released a studio album and a live double album in 1974 on which label in the UK?
4. Which Four Tops top three UK hit was written and given to them by the Moody Blues?
5. Which was the only case in the 1970s of the title of a Top 10 single, and the name of the artist, both being palindromes (spelt the same back to front)?
6. Which guitarist replaced Ritchie Blackmore in Deep Purple in 1975?
7. Who was the vocalist of Generation X?
8. Which South African act had a No. 2 in 1978 with *Substitute*?
9. Which rock-jazz fusion band included Alexis Korner and Peter Thorup on joint lead vocals?
10. By what name was John Mellor better known?
11. Which song begins with the following lyrics: 'Glossy grey magician sitting lotus on the floor, Belly dancing beauty with a power driven saw'?
12. Which No. 1 hit in 1978 celebrated the artist L.S. Lowry?
13. Who played keyboards with the Strawbs, had previously been a member of Amen Corner, and also played with the Bee Gees on their contributions to the *Saturday Night Fever* soundtrack album?

14. Which group included guitarists Gary Roberts and Gerry Cott?
15. Which was the first Sweet hit to be written by the group themselves?
16. What was Cher's only Top 10 hit of the decade?
17. In the US, two singles were released from George Harrison's triple album *All Things Must Pass*, and both were hits; which was the second?
18. Who co-wrote *Mull of Kintyre* with Paul McCartney?
19. Which Jim Webb song, which had been a major hit in 1968 for actor Richard Harris, was also recorded with some success in the 1970s by Donna Summer and also by the Four Tops?
20. What was the No. 1 Christmas single in 1971?
21. Which musical instrument not normally associated with rock music is featured on *Are You Ready To Rock* by Wizzard and *It's a Long Way To The Top (If You Wanna Rock'n'Roll)* by AC/DC?
22. Which title, though different songs in each case, gave minor hits to T. Rex in 1976 and After The Fire in 1979?
23. How many UK Top 10 hits did Cliff Richard have in the 1970s?
24. Who had hits with *That Same Old Feeling* and *It's Like A Sad Old Kinda Movie*?
25. What was the inspiration for Gilbert O'Sullivan's No. 1 hit *Clair*?
26. Who had hits with cover versions of *Come Back My Love* and *Reet Petite*?
27. Who sang vocals on hits by Edison Lighthouse, White Plains, the Pipkins and First Class?

28. Which group once claimed that if they moved next door, your lawn would die?
29. Which Motown band had their first UK Top 20 hit in 1974 with the instrumental *Machine Gun?*
30. Al Stewart had two US Top 10 hits in the 1970s. One was *The Year of the Cat*; what was the other?
31. Two acts covered Dusty Springfield's debut hit *I Only Want To Be With You*, and like the original, they peaked at No. 4. Name one of them.
32. *Fire* was the Pointer Sisters' first UK Top 30 hit – who wrote it?
33. Who briefly replaced Allan Clarke as the Hollies' vocalist, between 1972 and 1973?
34. Before Gallagher & Lyle found success as a recording duo in their own right, of which early 1970s group were they an integral part?
35. *Re-make/Re-Model* and *Bitters End* were the first and last tracks on whose debut album?
36. *Looks Looks Looks* by Sparks featured backing vocals by which late 1960s chart-topping singer?
37. Which actor and comedian had a novelty hit in 1978 with *Loving You Has Made Me Bananas?*
38. Who made his chart debut in 1977 with a cover of *Do Wah Diddy Diddy?*
39. What was the title of David Bowie's 1973 collection of cover versions?
40. Only two acts entered the UK singles chart at No. 1 in the first week of release during this decade; name either.
41. Which 1980s solo artist made his chart debut in 1978 on the Streetband hit *Toast*?

42. Which instrumental UK hit in 1970, peaking at No. 2, was the brainchild of pianist and arranger Zak Lawrence, and featured Harry Pitch on harmonica?
43. The Stranglers' first UK Top 10 hit was a double A-side. *Peaches* was one track; what was the other?
44. What marketing feat was responsible for the Cars' *My Best Friend's Girl* entering the UK Top 10 in its first week of release in 1978?
45. Which well-known British drummer died in September 1978?
46. What was the name of John Peel's record label, said to have been named after his hamster, and which was wound up at the end of 1972 (the label, not the hamster)?
47. By what name were the duo of John Fiddler and Peter Hope-Evans better known?
48. Who had Top 10 hits as a member of Stealers Wheel and later as a solo artist?
49. What did Johnny Thunders and Tom Petty have in common?
50. *Girls Talk* was a hit for Dave Edmunds in 1979, but who wrote it?

Answers

1. Boney M
2. Barry White
3. Island
4. *Simple Game*
5. *SOS,* ABBA
6. Tommy Bolin
7. Billy Idol
8. Clout
9. CCS

10. Joe Strummer (the Clash)
11. *Lady Eleanor*, Lindisfarne
12. *Matchstalk Men and Matchstalk Cats and Dogs*, Brian and Michael
13. Blue Weaver
14. Boomtown Rats
15. *Fox on the Run*
16. *Gypsies, Tramps And Thieves*
17. *What is Life*
18. Denny Laine
19. *Mcarthur Park*
20. *Ernie (the Fastest Milkman in the West)*, Benny Hill
21. Bagpipes
22. *Laser Love*
23. 4
24. Pickettywitch
25. Clair was the daughter of his manager Gordon Mills, for whom he used to babysit
26. Darts
27. Tony Burrows
28. Motorhead
29. Commodores
30. *Time Passages*
31. The Bay City Rollers, The Tourists
32. Bruce Springsteen
33. Michael Rickfors
34. McGuinness Flint
35. Roxy Music
36. Mary Hopkin
37. Guy Marks
38. Andrew Gold
39. *Pin-Ups*
40. Slade, Gary Glitter (both in 1973)
41. Paul Young
42. *Groovin' with Mr Bloe*, Mr Bloe
43. *Go Buddy Go*

44. It was the first single widely available as a picture disc
45. Keith Moon
46. Dandelion
47. Medicine Head
48. Gerry Rafferty
49. Their backing bands were called the Heartbreakers
50. Elvis Costello

The 70s – Part 2

1. What was the first hit on the Two-Tone label?
2. Which group was initially called Smile?
3. Born Bernard Jewry, he had hits in the 1960s as Shane Fenton and in the 1970s under which name?
4. Which guitarist did Ron Wood replace in the Rolling Stones?
5. Which James Bond movie theme was a hit for Carly Simon?
6. Which album launched the Virgin record label in 1973 and had the catalogue number V2001?
7. Which keyboard player left Status Quo in 1971?
8. Which white Canadian singer had two top ten hits on the Tamla Motown label?
9. What was the Eagles' only UK Top 10 single?
10. What was Wishbone Ash's only Top 10 album?
11. *Dancing in the Moonlight* was a hit for Toploader many years later, but who took the song into the US Top 20 in 1973?
12. *Without You* by Nilsson was written by Pete Ham and Tom Evans of which group?
13. Who sang vocals on Cozy Powell's *Na Na Na*?
14. For who was it *Four In the Morning* in 1972?
15. What was the best-selling album in the UK during the 1970s?
16. Gwen's husband had his greatest success with songs written and produced by Casey and Finch – who was he?

17. Which Canadian group toured Europe in 1979 and had their only Top 50 UK hit that year with *Paradise Skies?*
18. Which 1970s chart-topper has also been a No. 1 since the decade for Doctor and the Medics, and for Gareth Gates?
19. What was Ian Hunter's only Top 20 solo single?
20. What do the following 1970s hits have in common: *If You Leave Me Now, More Than a Feeling, Carry on Wayward Son*?
21. Apart from Roy Wood, who played cello for both Electric Light Orchestra and Wizzard?
22. Which man, convicted for murder in 1884, was the subject of Fairport Convention's 1971 concept album *The Man They Couldn't Hang*?
23. Which group was formed by Midge Ure, Glen Matlock, Rusty Egan and Steve New?
24. Which singer-songwriter took his own life on 9 April 1976?
25. Which Leonard Cohen album was produced by Phil Spector?
26. Which was Bob Marley & the Wailers' first UK hit single?
27. *Pacific Ocean Blue*, released in 1977, was the only solo album from which drummer in which group?
28. Which Pink Floyd album was the soundtrack to the film *La Vallee*, by Barbet Schroeder?
29. Which soul group was fronted by 'General' Norman Johnson?
30. Who co-starred with the Bee Gees in the ill-fated film of *Sergeant Pepper's Lonely Hearts Club Band* in 1978?
31. Why was 1979 a good summer for people called Webb?
32. Who were Debra, Joan, Kim and Kathie?

33. Who designed the Rolling Stones' *Sticky Fingers* album sleeve?
34. Actor Gary Holton fronted which 1970s group?
35. Which British-based American female singer, renowned for her pigtails, had previously had a career recording screams for horror movies?
36. Who had more UK Top 10 hits in the 1970s, the Carpenters or the Stylistics?
37. Who was lead vocalist with Nazareth?
38. Which of the Goodies wrote their hits?
39. The riff from the Horace Silver jazz standard *Song for my Father* was used in which 1970s minor hit?
40. In September 1975, three different versions of which Rolling Stones song, including one by the group themselves (or to be more accurate, by one of them plus session musicians), made the lower reaches of the Top 50?
41. Which word is relative to the Smurfs and Chicory Tip?
42. Carl Wayne, formerly of The Move, was offered a song in 1974 which he rejected as 'rubbish', and the songwriters proceeded to create a session group around it. The result was a No. 1 – name the group and song.
43. Who was the only female singer to have two No. 1s in the 1970s (not counting Olivia Newton-John, whose hits were duets with John Travolta)?
44. Whose greatest success in the singles and album charts was with *All Around My Hat*?
45. *Elizabethan Reggae* was a hit in 1970, but at first incorrectly credited to Byron Lee. To whom was the credit changed after a few weeks?

46. Who recorded the albums 'Flashes from the Archives of Oblivion' and 'Bullinamingvase'?
47. Which group was fronted by vocalist Phil Mogg?
48. What was the Tremeloes' final Top 40 entry?
49. Springwater had a Top 10 instrumental hit in 1971, but what was the name of the musician who wrote it and played all the instruments?
50. Which group featured two of its four members simultaneously playing both sides of a nickelodeon?

Answers

1. *Gangsters*, The Specials
2. Queen
3. Alvin Stardust
4. Mick Taylor
5. *Nobody Does It Better* (movie, *The Spy Who Loved Me*)
6. 'Tubular Bells', Mike Oldfield
7. Roy Lynes
8. R. Dean Taylor
9. *Hotel California*
10. 'Argus'
11. King Harvest
12. Badfinger
13. Frank Aiello
14. Faron Young
15. 'Bridge over Troubled Water', Simon & Garfunkel
16. George McCrae
17. Max WEebster
18. *Spirit in the Sky*, Norman Greenbaum
19. *Once Bitten Twice Shy*

20. The groups who recorded them were named after American cities – Chicago, Boston, Kansas
21. Hugh McDowell
22. John 'Babbacombe' Lee
23. Rich Kids
24. Phil Ochs
25. 'Death of a Ladies' Man'
26. *No Woman No Cry*
27. Dennis Wilson, of the Beach Boys
28. 'Obscured By Clouds'
29. Chairmen of the Board
30. Peter Frampton
31. Cliff Richard (real name Harry Webb) and Gary Numan (real name Gary Webb) had back-to-back No. 1 singles in August and September (*We Don't Talk Anymore*, *Cars*)
32. Sister Sledge
33. Andy Warhol
34. Heavy Metal Kids
35. Lene Lovich
36. The Stylistics (10); the Carpenters had 7
37. Dan McCafferty
38. Bill Oddie
39. *Rikki Don't Lose That Number*, Steely Dan
40. *Out of Time*
41. Father (*Son of my Father*; Father Abraham)
42. *Sugar Baby Love*, The Rubettes
43. Suzi Quatro
44. Steeleye Span
45. Boris Gardiner (who was mis-spelt Boris Gardner at first – they never got it right)
46. Roy Harper
47. UFO
48. *Hello Buddy*
49. Phil Cordell
50. Sailor

The 80s – Part 1

1. Which chart-topping duo had an exclamation mark at the end of their name?
2. What was the first song played at Live Aid on 13 July 1985?
3. Which song gave Kylie and Jason a No. 1 as a duo early in 1989?
4. Which ABBA single was officially released in the UK only as a 12”? (Note, some import copies on 7” on another label were readily on sale at the same time)
5. What was the title of Rockpile’s only album?
6. Who was the only artist to have at least one UK Top 75 hit every year of the 1980s?
7. KD, Jazz and Silver Spinner were members of which American rap group who had a Top 10 UK hit in 1987?
8. Which single spent 38 weeks on the chart in 1983 and 1984 although it was only released on 12”?
9. Which Beatles album was released in 1982 but failed to make the UK album chart?
10. What was the second best-selling single in the UK during the 1980s?
11. Who had hit singles in the 1980s singing duets with Olivia Newton-John, Elton John, Van Morrison and Sarah Brightman?
12. Which 1987 chart-topping one-hit wonder was a collaboration between the bands A.R. Kane and Colourbox?
13. Which Duran Duran spin-off charted in 1985 with *Some Like It Hot* and *Get It On*?

14. What were the Christian names of B.A. Robertson?
15. Which Ian Dury single was banned by the BBC in 1981 on the grounds of bad taste?
16. Which was the first Stock-Aitken-Waterman production to top the UK singles chart?
17. Who presented *Juke Box Jury* when it returned to the BBC schedules for a short run in 1989 and again in 1990?
18. Which member of 10cc produced Agnetha Faltskog's 'Eyes Of A Woman' album and co-wrote several tracks with Paul McCartney on the 'Press To Play' album?
19. Which Journey single was only a minor British hit in 1982 on its first appearance, but gave them a Top 10 hit in 2009 thanks to exposure via a cover version on *The X Factor* on TV?
20. On the chart of 17 August 1985, which female singer held the two top positions in the UK singles chart?
21. What was the name of Bruce Hornsby's band?
22. Which female vocalist had hit duets with Joe Cocker and Bill Medley, and was the first artist to make the charts with a song by Leonard Cohen?
23. Who were *Living After Midnight, Breaking the Law* and then *United* in 1980?
24. Which group had their greatest UK successes with the albums 'Eliminator' and 'Afterburner'?
25. Who produced the Pogues' album 'Rum, Sodomy And The Lash'?
26. Which female actress turned singer made videos for two of her Top 10 hits, one including an appearance from Paul McCartney and another with Neil Kinnock?

27. Prior to being released as a single, *Walk Of Life* had been the B-side of which earlier Dire Straits hit?
28. Who enjoyed a hit with a cover version of Bruce Springsteen's *Dancing In the Dark* in 1985?
29. What was the first No. 1 by Jive Bunny and the Mastermixers?
30. Frankie Goes To Hollywood and Huey Lewis and the News, and which female vocalist, all had major hits with different songs called *The Power Of Love* between 1984 and 1985?
31. Dennis Waterman's 1980 hit *I Could Be So Good For You* was the theme tune of his popular ITV series, but what was the title?
32. Who sang the first line on Band Aid's *Do They Know It's Christmas* (the original 1984 version)?
33. Who sang backing vocals on Steve Winwood's *Higher Love*?
34. In 1983 ATF (After The Fire) had an American top five hit with which single which only just made the British Top 50?
35. *Masterblaster* by Stevie Wonder was a tribute to whom?
36. Which radio and TV music presenter had previously been Billy Bragg's roadie?
37. In which year was the first of the 'Now That's What I Call Music' albums released?
38. Which chart-topping disco hit of 1980 was written and originally recorded by Ray Dorset and Mungo Jerry?
39. Which song from the move *Buster*, a cover version of a No. 2 hit in 1966, topped the charts for Phil Collins in 1988?

40. Which single by George Michael was still a top five hit despite being banned by daytime radio because the title was deemed offensive?
41. Who revived the Supremes' *You Keep Me Hangin' On* and was rewarded with a No. 2 UK, No. 1 US hit in the late 1980s?
42. To which group did Ray Parker Jr pay an out-of-court settlement for plagiarizing one of their hits for *Ghostbusters*?
43. Which Gene Pitney hit of the 1960s topped the chart in 1989 when he re-recorded it as a duet with Marc Almond?
44. Who was a one-hit wonder in 1988 with *The First Time*?
45. Originally a hit nine years earlier for Harold Melvin and the Blue Notes, and Thelma Houston, which song gave the Communards the biggest hit of their career in 1986?
46. At which festival in summer 1988 were two people killed during a set by Guns'n'Roses?
47. What was the only Top 20 hit by Rush?
48. Which former vocalist of Generation X enjoyed greater success as a soloist?
49. *A Touch Of Grey* was the first US Top 10 single for which long-established group?
50. Which former punk guitarist topped the charts in 1982 with a song from *South Pacific*?

Answers

1. Wham!
2. *Rockin' All Over the World,* Status Quo
3. *Especially For You*
4. *Lay All Your Love On Me*
5. 'Seconds Of Pleasure'
6. Diana Ross

7. Whistle
8. *Blue Monday,* New Order
9. 'Reel Music'
10. *Relax*, Frankie Goes To Hollywood
11. Cliff Richard
12. MARRS
13. The Power Station
14. Bryan Alexander
15. *Spasticus Autisticus*
16. *You Spin Me Round (Like A Record),* Dead or Alive
17. Jools Holland
18. Eric Stewart
19. *Don't Stop Believin'*
20. Madonna
21. The Range
22. Jennifer Warnes
23. Judas Priest
24. ZZ Top
25. Elvis Costello
26. Tracey Ullman
27. *So Far Away*
28. Big Daddy
29. *Swing The Mood*
30. Jennifer Rush
31. *Minder*
32. Paul Young
33. Chaka Khan
34. *Der Kommissar*
35. Bob Marley
36. Andy Kershaw
37. 1983
38. *Feels Like I'm In Love*
39. *A Groovy Kind Of Love*
40. *I Want Your Sex*
41. Kim Wilde
42. Huey Lewis and the News

43. *Something's Gotten Hold of my Heart*
44. Robin Beck
45. *Don't Leave Me This Way*
46. Castle Donington Monsters of Rock Festival
47. *The Spirit Of Radio*
48. Billy Idol
49. Grateful Dead
50. Captain Sensible (with *Happy Talk*)

The 80s – Part 2

1. After The Beat disbanded, Andy Cox and David Steele helped to form which equally successful band?
2. What was the debut single by Heaven 17, initially banned by the BBC for its politically controversial content?
3. Which male vocalist had had minor success with Streetband and the Q-Tips, but far more as a soloist from 1983 onwards?
4. Who had the best-selling album in the UK of 1981 with 'Kings of the Wild Frontier'?
5. Which group helped Sandie Shaw to a comeback in 1984 with *Hand in Glove*?
6. Eddi Reader was lead vocalist with which chart-topping group?
7. What was Def Leppard's first UK Top 10 single?
8. Who produced Bonnie Tyler's 'Faster Than the Speed of Light'?
9. A cover version of *That's The Way I Like It* by KC and the Sunshine Band gave which group their first UK hit?
10. Which single gave Roy Orbison a top three hit only a few weeks after his death?
11. Who played drums with Culture Club?
12. What was the title of Simple Minds' live album released in 1987?
13. Who co-wrote USA for Africa's *We Are the World* with Michael Jackson?
14. Which was the first single of the 1980s to enter the UK chart at No. 1?

15. Motorhead and Girlschool joined forces to have a top five hit in 1981 with which old rock'n'roll classic?
16. Which solo star had previously fronted Bronski Beat and the Communards?
17. Two acts reached No. 2 in 1981 with different songs called *Happy Birthday*. One was Stevie Wonder; who was the other?
18. Which Frank Sinatra single, first released as a single in 1980, was reactivated to give him a UK Top 10 hit in 1986?
19. In the mid-1980s, which soundtrack album topped the US charts for 24 weeks?
20. Which Europop single, a minor hit for Jonathan King in 1979, gave Laura Branigan a transatlantic Top 10 hit in 1982-3?
21. Which cover version of a hit for Elvis Presley in the 1970s became the Christmas No. 1 of 1987?
22. *State of Shock* was a hit in 1984 for the Jacksons and which British vocalist?
23. Which song gave Toto a US No. 1 and UK top three hit in 1983?
24. Who replaced David Lee Roth as vocalist with Van Halen in 1985?
25. Which Nat King Cole song was covered by Rick Astley in 1987, with both versions simultaneously in the Top 10 at Christmas?
26. Duran Duran first attracted attention as the opening act for which female singer on tour late in 1980?
27. Which Tom Petty solo album from 1989 is sometimes regarded as a follow-up to the first Traveling Wilburys album, as it features all of the group except for Bob Dylan?
28. Which band did Mick Jones form in 1984 after being sacked from the Clash?

29. Which Billy Joel album contained the singles Pressure, Allentown, and Goodnight Saigon?
30. Which trio released the album 'Licensed to Ill' in 1986, reviewed by *Rolling Stone* magazine under the heading, 'Three Idiots Create a Masterpiece'?
31. Who contributed backing vocals to David Cassidy's *The Last Kiss* and Elton John's *Nikita* in 1985?
32. Which was John Cougar's only US chart-topping album of the decade (and his only one to date)?
33. Which Daryl Hall & John Oates hit of 1983 had been a minor UK hit for Mike Oldfield the previous year?
34. Which Billie Holliday song gave Alison Moyet her most successful UK hit?
35. Joan Jett & the Blackhearts' *I Love Rock'n'Roll* had been recorded in the 1970s by which British group?
36. Released in 1981, 'Hoy-Hoy!' was a compilation album of live and studio material by which US band, whose front man had died suddenly two years earlier?
37. Which was the Hooters' only UK Top 30 hit?
38. *Oops Upside Your Head*, often known at discos as 'the rowing song', was the most successful UK hit for which group?
39. Which title, but different songs, gave Blondie a No. 1 in 1980 and Spagna a No. 2 seven years later?
40. After an edition of *The Big Time* on BBC TV, hosted by Esther Rantzen, which previously unknown female singer who who was featured had her first two singles simultaneously in the Top 10?

41. Although it failed in the UK, which single gave Boston a US No. 1 in 1986?
42. *Stainsby Girls* was whose first UK Top 30 hit?
43. Which female rock group, formed in Minnesota around 1981, had their greatest successes at the end of the decade with *On the Edge of a Broken Heart* and *Cryin'*?
44. Although 'Bat Out of Hell' by Meat Loaf has rarely been out of the UK album chart since its release in 1978, in which year did it first reach the Top 10 for one week – at No. 9?
45. Which album did George Martin produce for UFO?
46. *Down Under* and 'Business as Usual' topped the singles and album chart simultaneously in 1983 for which group?
47. Erasure reached No. 2 in 1988 with the EP 'Crackers International'; which was the main track, which received the most airplay?
48. Who was the founder of Casablanca Records, who died of cancer in 1982 at the age of 39?
49. Steve 'Silk' Hurley had the first house music No. 1 single in the UK chart, without any prior exposure on Radio 1 – what was the title?
50. Which record label was set up by UB40 in 1980 after they left Graduate Records?

Answers

1. Fine Young Cannibals
2. *(We Don't Need This) Fascist Groove Thang*
3. Paul Young
4. Adam and the Ants
5. The Smiths
6. Fairground Attraction

7. *Animal*
8. Jim Steinman
9. Dead or Alive
10. *You Got It*
11. Jon Moss
12. 'Live in the City of Light'
13. Lionel Richie
14. *Going Underground*, The Jam
15. *Please Don't Touch*
16. Jimmy Somerville
17. Altered Images
18. *Theme from New York, New York*
19. *Purple Rain*, Prince
20. *Gloria*
21. *Always On My Mind*, Pet Shop Boys
22. Mick Jagger
23. *Africa*
24. Sammy Hagar
25. *When I Fall in Love*
26. Hazel O'Connor
27. 'Full Moon Fever'
28. B.A.D. (Big Audio Dynamite)
29. 'The Nylon Curtain'
30. The Beastie Boys
31. George Michael
32. 'American Fool'
33. *Family Man*
34. *That Ole Devil Called Love*
35. The Arrows
36. Little Feat
37. *Satellite*
38. The Gap Band
39. *Call Me*
40. Sheena Easton
41. *Amanda*
42. Chris Rea
43. Vixen

44. 1981. (It also spent two consecutive weeks at No. 9 in 1993)
45. 'No Place to Run'
46. Men at Work
47. *Stop!*
48. Neil Bogart
49. *Jack Your Body*
50. DEP International

The 90s

1. What was the title of England New Order's 1990 No. 1 World Cup hit?
2. Why were Milli Vanilli stripped of their Grammy award in 1990?
3. Which was Nirvana's only top five hit of the decade?
4. Whose life was commemorated in a tribute concert at Wembley on 20 April 1992?
5. In 1990 Robert Van Winkle was dubbed the Elvis of Rap, but under what name was he better known?
6. Which comedian collaborated with the Wonder Stuff on a chart-topping revival of *Dizzy*?
7. Which song by Argent, with a slightly modified title, gave Kiss a No. 4 hit in January 1992?
8. Which member of the Corrs played fiddle?
9. Who entered the charts at No. 1 in 1997 with *Mmmbop*?
10. *Tears In Heaven* was co-written by Eric Clapton and Will Jennings in memory of whom?
11. Which chart-topping singer in 1991 was the son of the bassist whose group had a No. 1 in 1967?
12. Which hit sampled the Andrew Oldham Orchestra's version of *The Last Time* by the Rolling Stones?
13. To which producer was Shania Twain married from 1993 to 2010?
14. What was Sheryl Crow's first charting album?

15. Who was successively vocalist with Goodbye Mr Mackenzie and Garbage?
16. Which band was formed by Dave Grohl after Nirvana?
17. What was Steps' first Top 10 single?
18. Which blues guitarist guested on one track on the second Traveling Wilburys album?
19. By what name is Richard Melville Hall better known?
20. Who had hits with *Line Up, Connection* and *Waking Up*?
21. Where was the Silver Clef Award Winners concert staged in June 1990?
22. Which group featured Richard and Fred Fairbrass?
23. On the 1998 Top three hit *I'm Your Angel*, which singer was credited jointly with Celine Dion?
24. The video for Shania Twain's *Man! I Feel Like A Woman* was a spoof of the video for *Addicted To Love* by whom?
25. Andy McCluskey, who founded Atomic Kitten, was a member of which synth-pop act?
26. Who was the featured vocalist on the 1992 Santana hit *Smooth*?
27. Who charted with a cover version of the Small Faces' *Itchycoo Park* in 1995?
28. In which journal did Heart Management place an advertisement in February 1994 which resulted in the formation of the Spice Girls?
29. Which British singer headlined the North Stage on the last night of Woodstock '94 and closed the festival?
30. Eddie Vedder is guitarist and vocalist with which band?

31. Who produced Elton John's *Candle in the Wind '97*, performed at the funeral of Diana Princess of Wales?
32. Primal Scream won the first Mercury Music Prize in 1992, with which album?
33. Which jazz singer and musician had a posthumous Top 10 in 1994 with a song which had originally been a James Bond movie theme?
34. Which band was fronted by singer Sonya Madan?
35. When Edwin Starr had a minor hit with a remake of *War* in 1993, what was the full artist credit?
36. Which group's final album before disbanding was 'Construction For The Modern Idiot'?
37. Which Monkees oldie was successfully revived by EMF with Reeves and Mortimer in 1995?
38.Which two acts collaborated on the 1994 hit *Whatta Man?*
39. Which Doobie Brothers oldie, never a UK hit the first time round, was remixed and hit the Top 10 in 1993?
40. Which standard gave Jose Carreras, Placido Domingo and Luciano Pavarotti a Top 30 hit in 1998?
41. Who topped the chart in 1997 with *Professional Widow?*
42. Happy Mondays had a hit in 1990 with *Step On*, the same song but with an abbreviated title of a hit in 1971 for whom?
43. Which guitarist, best known for his work with David Bowie and Ian Hunter, died of cancer in 1993?
44. Which Randy Crawford oldie became a Top 10 hit for Shola Ama in 1997?

45. Which was Green Day's only UK Top 10 single of the decade?
46. Emilia, who had a Top five hit in 1998 with *Big Big World,* came from which country?
47. With whom did Status Quo collaborate on their 1996 Top 30 hit *Fun Fun Fun*?
48. Which previously unreleased Thin Lizzy track was a Top 40 hit for them in 1991?
49. What was the chart-topping charity single for Comic Relief in 1991 by Hale and Pace?
50. *If You Ever* was a hit in 1996 for East 17 in collaboration with which female singer?

Answers

1. *World In Motion*
2. It was revealed that they had not sung on their records
3. *Heart Shaped Box*
4. Freddie Mercury
5. Vanilla Ice
6. Vic Reeves
7. *God Gave Rock'n'Roll To You II*
8. Sharon
9. Hanson
10. Eric's young son Conor
11. Chesney Hawkes
12. *Bittersweet Symphony,* Verve
13. Robert John Lange
14. 'Tuesday Night Music Club'
15. Shirley Manson
16. The Foo Fighters
17. *The Last Thing On My Mind*
18. Gary Moore
19. Moby
20. Elastica

21. Knebworth Park
22. Right Said Fred
23. R. Kelly
24. Robert Palmer
25. OMD (Orchestral Manoeuvres in the Dark)
26. Rob Thomas
27. M People
28. *The Stage*
29. Peter Gabriel
30. Pearl Jam
31. Sir George Martin
32. Screamadelica
33. Louis Armstrong
34. Echobelly
35. Edwin Starr and Shadow
36. The Wonder Stuff
37. *I'm A Believer*
38. Salt'N'Pepa and En Vogue
39. *Long Train Runnin'*
40. *You'll Never Walk Alone*
41. Tori Amos
42. John Kongos
43. Mick Ronson
44. *You Might Need Somebody*
45. *Basket Case*
46. Sweden
47. The Beach Boys
48. *Dedication*
49. *The Stonk*
50. Gabrielle

The 21st century

1. Which double A-side was at No. 1 in the UK at the time of the new millennium?
2. Which was the first album by The Darkness, released in 2003?
3. Who in 2014 contributed *Who I Am* to the soundtrack of the Disney animated film *The Pirate Fairy*?
4. Which Los Angeles band originally formed in 1994 as Kara's Flowers?
5. Which veteran singer recorded *Islands In The Stream*, the No. 1 single in aid of Comic Relief in 2009, with Ruth Jones, Rob Brydon and Robin Gibb?
6. Which Rhianna single topped the UK charts for ten weeks in summer 2007?
7. Which group was formed in 2009 by Mick Jagger and Dave Stewart?
8. At which London venue did Coldplay begin their Viva La Vida tour in June 2008 with a free gig?
9. Which James Bond movie theme song was written and recorded by Adele in 2012?
10. Which record rose no higher than No. 18 in the charts in January 1972, but was reissued and became the best-selling single of 2005?
11. Dan Gillespie Seals is the vocalist and front man of which band?
12. Which Bob Dylan song was sampled by Gabrielle on her No. 1 hit *Rise*?
13. Who in 2008 became the first Welsh singer to top the UK charts for 25 years?

14. For which film based on a novel by one of the Brontë sisters did Mumford & Sons record the song *Enemy*?
15. Lily Allen's No. 1 *Somewhere Only We Know* was recorded originally as an advertisement for which department store?
16. Which group features the vocalists Jake Shears and Ana Mantronic?
17. Her real name is Jocelyn Eve Stoker, but by what name is she better known?
18. Which Michael Jackson song was a No. 1 hit in 2009 by the finalists of *The X-Factor*?
19. Which 42-year-old music TV programme came off the air in 2006?
20. Which group in February 2001 became the first western rock band to play in Cuba?
21. *When You Tell Me That You Love Me* by Westlife, a UK No. hit in 1995, also featured which female vocalist?
22. What was the title of Chrissie Hynde's first solo album, released in 2014?
23. Which rap metal band had the No. 1 UK single at Christmas 2009 with *Killing In The Name*?
24. Which singer was runner-up in the second series of *The X-Factor* in 2005 and represented the UK in the Eurovision Song Contest three years later?
25. 'These Streets', released in 2006, was whose debut album?
26. With whom did Robert Plant collaborate on the album 'Raising Sand'?
27. 'The Endless River', released in 2014, is expected to be the final album by which group?
28. With which American singer did Amy Winehouse duet on what was her final recording ever?

29. Which musical, opening at the Piccadilly Theatre in 2012, was based on the songs of the Spice Girls?
30. Of which group was Nicole Scherzinger a member before she joined the Pussycat Dolls?
31. What was Mika's follow-up Top 10 hit to his No. 1 *Grace Kelly*?
32. Which group had a No. 1 with *Sorry Seems To Be The Hardest Word* in 2002, featuring guest vocals by the original performer Elton John?
33. Which rapper also sometimes went under the alias Slim Shady?
34. Albert Hammond Jr, son of the songwriter Albert Hammond, is a member of which group?
35. Which singer won the first series of The X-Factor in 2004?
36. Which single by Leona Lewis went on to become the best-selling single of 2008 worldwide?
37. Which group had their first No. 1 album for 28 years in 2008 with 'Black Ice'?
38. Where was Michael Jackson preparing to play a series of British concerts at the time of his death in June 2009?
39. Who was the first unsigned artist to reach the UK top five through social networking sites alone with *Forever Yours*?
40. Which group would you associate with vocalist Gary Lightbody and guitarist Nathan Connolly?
41. Which Black-Eyed Peas single became the first, in 2006, to reach the Top 40 on downloads alone?
42. Which unsigned act had a UK No. 1 in 2013 with *Thrift Shop*?

43. Which album by One Direction made them the first UK group to debut at No. 1 in the US charts with their first album?
44. At which London venue did BBC Radio 2 stage a concert in September 2014 which was headlined by Jeff Lynne's ELO, with Blondie, Billy Ocean, Bellowhead and others as support?
45. Which 2014 hit by Oliver Heldens featuring Becky Hill became the last record to top the UK chart based on sales alone?
46. Which 2011 album was a collaboration between Lou Reed and Metallica?
47. Which group split in 2000, reformed in 2006, and released the album 'Zeitgeist' a year later?
48. Who released the albums 'Fearless', 'Speak Now' and 'Red'?
49. From which city do the Arctic Monkeys come?
50. By what name are Florence Welch and her group better known?

Answers

1. Westlife, *I Have A Dream/Seasons In The Sun*
2. 'Permission To Land'
3. Maroon 5
4. Natasha Bedingfield
5. Tom Jones
6. Umbrella
7. SuperHeavy
8. Brixton Academy
9. Skyfall
10. *Is This The Way To Amarillo*, Tony Christie
11. The Feeling

12. *Knockin' On Heaven's Door*
13. Duffy
14. *Wuthering Heights*
15. John Lewis
16. The Scissor Sisters
17. Joss Stone
18. *You Are Not Alone*
19. *Top Of The Pops*
20. Manic Street Preachers
21. Diana Ross (who had previously had a hit with the original, also reaching No. 2)
22. 'Stockholm'
23. Rage Against the Machine
24. Andy Abraham
25. Paolo Nutini
26. Alison Krauss
27. Pink Floyd
28. Tony Bennett
29. *Viva Forever*!
30. Eden's Crush
31. *Love Today*
32. Blue
33. Eminem
34. The Strokes
35. Steve Brookstein
36. *Bleeding Love*
37. AC/DC
38. O_2 Arena, London
39. Alex Day
40. Snow Patrol
41. *Pump It*
42. Macklemore and Ryan Lewis
43. 'Up All Night'
44. Hyde Park
45. *Gecko (Overdrive)*
46. *Lulu*
47. The Smashing Pumpkins

48. Taylor Swift
49. Sheffield
50. Florence and the Machine

Another Big Mix

In case the first hundred weren't enough, let's have another hundred. Like the rest of the book, these are mostly pop and rock, but with a few surprises to keep you on your toes.

1. In the BRIT Awards, what do these initials stand for?
2. Who was the Beatles' manager until his sudden death in 1967?
3. Who was known as the Thin White Duke?
4. Which American jazz record label was founded in 1939 by Alfred Lion and Max Margulis, and has been owned by the Universal Music Group since 2006?
5. What was the first album released by Simon & Garfunkel?
6. *5 Colours In Her Hair* was the debut hit single in 2004 by which band?
7. In which year did Bob Marley succumb to cancer?
8. Which progressive rock label was launched by EMI Records in the summer of 1969?
9. On the sleeve of the debut LP by McGuinness Flint, where in Devon did the photoshoot take place?
10. Ozzy Osbourne, Ronnie James Dio, and briefly Ian Gillan were successively vocalists in which group?
11. Which 1974 No. 1 single is generally regarded as the start of the disco era?

12. Which song was originally a hit for Tammy Wynette, but parodied more successfully a few months later by Billy Connolly?
13. Which day of the week was shared by hit titles by the Mamas and the Papas in the 1960s, the Boomtown Rats in the 1970s, and New Order and Bangles in the 1980s?
14. Whose albums included 'Quiet Life' and 'Gentlemen Take Polaroids'?
15. *Paradise Skies* was the only Top 50 UK hit for which Canadian group?
16. What was the name of Ian Dury's backing group?
17. Which two rock veterans teamed up for 'Going Back Home', a top three album in 2014?
18. Which record by Gary Puckett and the Union Gap topped the UK charts in 1968 and returned to the Top 10 six years later?
19. Who wrote and originally recorded *I Feel For You*, a No. 1 hit for Chaka Khan in 1984?
20. A Top 10 hit by Badfinger in 1972 and a No. 1 by Boyzone in 1998, although different songs, shared which title?
21. The Monkees had three No. 1 Billboard hits in the US. Which was the last?
22. Which record reached No. 2 in the UK first time round in 1975, and went back into the Top 10 in 1987 and 1997 as a remix and a reissue?
23. Glenn Tilbrook and Chris Difford were the songwriting partnership behind which group?
24. With which instrument would you have associated the jazz musicians Barney Kessel, Jim Raney and Tal Farlow?
25. What was Felice Taylor's only UK hit, a No. 11 in 1967?

26. Which title was shared by albums by the Temptations in 1969 and George Harrison in 1987?
27. Which frequently sung song was written by Patty and Mildred Hill around the end of the nineteenth century?
28. What is the name of the US National Anthem?
29. *Lifetime*, starring Yaya DaCosta, is a biopic of which singer?
30. Which late 60s group included Steve Stills and Neil Young in the line-up?
31. Which Finnish composer is best remembered for *Finlandia* and *Karelia Suite*?
32. The Capitol record label was founded in Los Angeles in which year?
33. Which was the only Beatles album to consist entirely of Lennon-McCartney compositions?
34. Which very successful mid-1970s group came from Carshalton?
35. Which Dave Edmunds hit was credited jointly to him and the Stray Cats?
36. Which was the only solo single by Judith Durham of The Seekers to make the UK Top 50?
37. Which legendary blues singer and guitarist, who died around 1938, was alleged to have made a pact with the devil?
38. Who was Gerry Rafferty's songwriting partner in Stealers Wheel?
39. Which Kinks song of 1968 was a hit in 1989 for Kirsty McColl – both coincidentally peaking at No. 12 in the UK?
40. Whose first two albums were 'The Kick Inside' and 'Lionheart'?
41. Which David Gates song topped the charts for Ken Boothe in 1974 and Boy George in 1987?

42. Of which group were Viv Stanshall, Neil Innes and Roger Ruskin Spear and Larry 'Legs' Smith members?
43. Which was the last operetta written by Gilbert & Sullivan, first performed in 1896?
44. A falsetto version of Bob Dylan's *Don't Think Twice, It's Alright*, a US hit in 1966, by the Four Seasons, was credited to who?
45. *Stand By Me* by B.B. King reached No. 1 on reissue in 1987, but in which year did it first make the UK Top 30?
46. Which film theme by Lulu was only a B-side in the UK, but a No. 1 in the US in 1967?
47. Which Desmond Dekker hit reached No. 1 in the UK in 1969 and returned to the top ten on reissue in 1975?
48. The guitarrón chileno (or Chilean guitar) does not have six strings – how many does it generally have?
49. Whose autobiography, completed after his death by his widow, was called *Margrave Of The Marshes?*
50. Excluding an unauthorised release, what was Van Morrison's first official solo album, issued in 1968?
51. Which American singer, also an actor, comedian, and film producer, was known as the King of Cool?
52. Which musical instrument was generally known until about 1770 as the hautbois, or French hoeboy?
53. Which Donna Summer record was initially banned as it was considered too suggestive for daytime broadcasting?
54. Which place name connects minor UK hit singles by Bob Seger and The Silver Bullet Band, Boz Scaggs and Thin Lizzy?

55. Which Geordie singer-songwriter and group leader released his first solo album 'Pipedream' and published a book of poems, *Mocking Horse,* both in 1973?

56. Which singer also appeared in the movies *Mad Max: Beyond Thunderdome, Tommy,* and *Last Action Hero*?

57. The Boswell Sisters are believed to be the first artistes to record a song called *Rock and Roll*, but in which year?

58. Which was the first UK TV programme to feature a performance from Bob Marley and The Wailers?

59. Who released the album 'Live Peace in Toronto 1969'?

60. Which song did Billy Joel write as a birthday present for his then wife Elizabeth?

61. On 23 October 1995, which British group achieved a new record when they played gigs in three continents, starting in Morocco, then London, finally Vancouver?

62. *My Heart Will Go On* by Celine Dion is the theme from which movie?

63. Which woman's name is the title of a 1968 hit by Tom Jones and part of a 1972 hit title by Middle Of The Road?

64. Which three instruments comprise a string trio?

65. What is the name of the ballroom dance in quadruple time which combines long and short steps in various sequences, and probably originated in North America in the early 20th century?

66. Which was the first solo album by Morrissey?

67. Which Radio 1 producer turned presenter had formerly been the trumpet player with The Alan Price Set?
68. Ralph Vaughan Williams was the first president of which organisation, formed in 1944 to protect composers' rights?
69. On the chart week ending 22 January 2005, which single became the UK's 1000th No. 1? (Clue – it was a double A-side Elvis Presley reissue)
70. Where did Fiddler's Dram take a day trip in 1979?
71. Which flower is named in titles of Top 10 hits by Marv Johnson, Mungo Jerry, and Elvis Costello?
72. Marc Almond and Dave Ball were members of which 1980s chart-topping duo?
73. Which record label featured in the title of a song recorded as an album track by Procol Harum (who not surprisingly recorded for that label at the time)?
74. Who was born in Long Branch, New Jersey, on 23 September 1949?
75. Which song topped the charts for Billy Ocean in 1986 and Boyzone in 1999?
76. When Terraplane disbanded in 1988, singer Danny Bowes and guitarist Luke Morley formed which more successful group?
77. Which song was a transatlantic hit for Roy Orbison as a soloist in 1961, and in 1992 after his death as a duet with k.d. lang?
78. Which traditional American folk song was a No. 1 hit for a group from north-east England on both sides of the Atlantic in 1964?
79. Which king of the buskers had two Top 10 hits in 1968?
80. Which record did Vera Lynn break in 2009?

81. In 2014 which group, in association with Apple Computers (not The Beatles' Apple), gave their new album away free of charge to everyone with an iTunes account?
82. Whose UK Top 40 chart career began in 1961 with *Runaway* and ended in 1965 with *Stranger In Town*?
83. Whose first singles were *What Makes You Beautiful* and *Gotta Be You*?
84. What in 1984 was the only UK Top 10 hit for China Crisis?
85. Which anti-war hit of 1965 by Barry McGuire was initially banned by the BBC?
86. Which drummer founded the Jazz Messengers in the late 1940s?
87. Which record was a hit, jointly, for Earth, Wind & Fire and the Emotions in 1979?
88. Tony Davis, Mick Groves, Cliff Hall, and Hughie Jones comprised which long-established English folk group?
89. Which song was a UK Top 10 hit for Maxine Nightingale in 1975 and Sinitta in 1989?
90. Who starred in the first 'talking picture', *The Jazz Singer*, in 1927?
91. Which song by Free was a Top 20 hit three times during the 1970s and again in 1991, reaching the Top 10 on two of those occasions?
92. Which record was the first single to be released on Warner Brothers in the UK, and topped the chart for eight weeks in 1960?
93. Which guitarist left the James Gang in 1975 to join the Eagles?
94. Which Christmas carol (English title required) was composed by Franz Gruber to lyrics by Joseph Mohr, and received its first performance at a church on Christmas Eve 1818?

95. *Freak Like Me* by Sugababes sampled which former No. 1?
96. Which conductor was regarded as the most successful album act before The Beatles, and the first act to sell over one million stereo albums, with six albums simultaneously in the US Top 30 in 1959?
97. What was the only British hit for John Fred and his Playboy Band?
99. Who had an US No. 1 and a UK No. 2 in 1991 with *More Than Words*?
100. Who had a minor UK hit in 1965 with *Witches Brew*, was later imprisoned after convicted of charges connected with prostitution, and immortalised in song by the Clash?

Answers

1. British Record Industry Trust
2. Brian Epstein
3. David Bowie
4. Blue Note
5. 'Wednesday Morning 3 a.m.'
6. McFly
7. 1981
8. Harvest
9. Brentor, on southern Dartmoor (Brentor church is visible in the extended picture to the left of the group)
10. Black Sabbath
11. *Rock Your Baby*
12. DIVORCE
13. Monday
14. Japan
15. Max Webster

16. The Blockheads
17. Roger Daltrey and Wilko Johnson
18. *Young Girl*
19. Prince
20. *No Matter What*
21. *Daydream Believer*
22. *You Sexy Thing*, Hot Chocolate
23. Squeeze
24. Guitar
25. *I Feel Love Comin' On*
26. 'Cloud Nine'
27. *Happy Birthday To You*
28. *The Star Spangled Banner*
29. Whitney Houston
30. Buffalo Springfield
31. Sibelius
32. 1942
33. 'A Hard Day's Night'
34. Mud
35. *The Race Is On*
36. *The Olive Tree*
37. Robert Johnson
38. Joe Egan
39. *Days*
40. Kate Bush
41. *Everything I Own*
42. The Bonzo Dog Band
43. *The Grand Duke*
44. The Wonder Who
45. 1961
46. *To Sir With Love*
47. *Israelites*
48. 24 or 25
49. John Peel
50. 'Astral Weeks'
51. Dean Martin
52. Oboe

53. *Love To Love You Baby*
54. Hollywood (*Hollywood Nights, Hollywood, Hollywood (Down On Your Luck)*)
55. Alan Hull (of Lindisfarne)
56. Tina Turner
57. 1934
58. *The Old Grey Whistle Test*
59. The Plastic Ono Band
60. *Just The Way You Are*
61. Def Leppard
62. *Titanic*
63. Delilah
64. Violin, viola, cello
65. Foxtrot
66. 'Viva Hate'
67. John Walters
68. The Composers' Guild of Great Britain
69. *One Night/I Got Stung*
70. Bangor
71. Rose
72. Soft Cell
73. Regal Zonophone (the song was *Magdalene, my Regal Zonophone*)
74. Bruce Springsteen
75. *When the Going Gets Tough, the Tough Get Going*
76. Thunder
77. *Crying*
78. *The House of the Rising Sun,* The Animals
79. Don Partridge
80. She became the eldest person ever to top the album chart, with the compilation *We'll Meet Again*
81. U2
82. Del Shannon
83. One Direction
84. *Wishful Thinking*

85. *Eve of Destruction*
86. Art Blakey
87. *Boogie Wonderland*
88. The Spinners
89. *Right Back Where We Started From*
90. Al Jolson
91. *All Right Now*
92. *Cathy's Clown*, The Everly Brothers
93. Joe Walsh
94. *Silent Night*
95. *Are Friends Electric*, Tubeway Army
96. Mantovani
97. *Judy in Disguise (With Glasses)*
98 *Les Misérables*
99. Extreme
100. Janie Jones

The Classics

The highbrow bit starts here, although there are just a couple of small nods to popular music along the way in this round.

1. Who was the first Master of the King's Musick, appointed in 1625?
2. In an orchestra, which instruments are placed behind the horns and trumpets?
3. To whom did Beethoven originally dedicate his Symphony No 3, the 'Eroica'?
4. Which institution has its headquarters at Kneller Hall, Middlesex?
5. By what name or nickname is Tchaikovsky's Symphony No 6 in B minor, Op 74, known?
6. Which festival in Suffolk was founded by Benjamin Britten in 1948?
7. Which musical era lasted from around 1600 to 1750?
8. Which composer wrote the music for *Land of Hope and Glory*?
9. The Three Choirs Festival rotates between Gloucester, Hereford and which other city?
10. Which bodily affliction was common to composers Beethoven, Fauré, Smetana, and percussionist Evelyn Glennie?
11. Which composer was nicknamed *il Prete Rosso* ('The Red Priest') because of his red hair?
12. Which Top 10 popular song from the 1970s includes the lyrics, 'She's sweet on Wagner, I think she'd die for Beethoven'?
13. Who composed *The Mask of Orpheus* and *The Triumph of Time*?

14. Which term was coined by Charles Burney in 1805 to describe music not intended for church, theatre or public concert room, but rather for string quartets and ensemble music by small groups?
15. Whose *Symphony No. 3*, written in 1976, is also known as the Symphony of Sorrowful Songs?
16. Baroque music takes its name from the Portuguese word barroco, meaning what?
17. Milan Opera House, built in 1778, is known as La Scala – what does the name literally mean?
18. Which composer went mad and was confined in the lunatic asylum at Prague where he died in 1884?
19. The earliest extant example of which instrument was built in 1744 by Gaetano Vinaccia and can be found in the Conservatoire Royal de Musique in Brussels?
20. In which country was the conductor Yehudi Menhuin born?
21. Who wrote *Concierto di Aranjuez*?
22. What is the name given to male sopranos who were castrated before puberty in order to preserve their voices?
23. *Zadok the Priest* was written as a coronation anthem by which composer?
24. The military march *Liberty Bell* by Sousa was adopted as the theme tune for which popular TV series?
25. Which composer tried to drown himself in the river Neva, Russia, in 1877?
26. Which composer was born on 22 May 1813 at Leipzig?
27. In which city in 1857 did Sir Charles Halle found the orchestra which bears his name?

28. Who composed *New World Symphony*?

29. Which great music reference work was founded by Sir George Grove?

30. After which event did Rachmaninov leave Russia for the last time?

31. What is the name given to a choral composition, generally on a sacred text?

32. In which year was Beethoven's 9th Symphony given its world premiere?

33. Whose *Symphony No. 9* was partly inspired by Thomas Hardy's *Tess Of the D'Urbervilles* and given its premiere in April 1958, four months before the composer's death?

34. After an approach from Malcolm Sargent, which conductor founded the London Philharmonic Orchestra in 1932 and became its first conductor, but after differences with the players founded the rival Royal Philharmonic Orchestra in 1946?

35. Which 19th century composer died in Leipzig, it was said, as a marching band passed by his home, a servant opened the front door, the music was clearly heard throughout the house, he sat up in his bed as if to conduct, then fell back lifeless against the pillows?

36. A short extract from The 'Troika', from Prokoviev's *Lieutenant Kijé Suite,* was used in which major 1975 Christmas hit single?

37. What is the name generally given to the British army bugle call normally played at military funerals?

38. Which composer was appointed organist of the Chapel Royal in 1682?

39. Which poet collaborated with Benjamin Britten on *Hymn to St Cecilia*?

40. Who was the artistic director of the Vienna State Opera from 1957 to 1964 and regularly

conducted the Berlin and Vienna Philharmonic orchestras until shortly before his death in 1989?

41. What is the colloquial term used for what happens when the parts in an ensemble collide because the musicians are not playing together?

42. Which Austrian concert pianist was successively married to a grandson of King George V and, after their divorce, to a former leader of the British Liberal Party?

43. Where in London did Dame Myra Hess found and direct a series of lunchtime music rehearsals during the Second World War?

44. Which King of Bavaria, remembered for his extravagantly-built castles, was also the main patron of Richard Wagner?

45. Which Russian instrument of the lute family has three strings, a triangular belly, and moveable frets on the arm?

46. Which term is applied to a period of great emotional intensity in German literature and music, around 1760-1780?

47. What is the name of a musical ensemble from Indonesia, chiefly from the islands of Bali and Java, usually featuring instruments including xylophones, drums, gongs and bamboo flutes?

48. What is the name often given to Mozart's Piano Concerto No. 21 because it was used as the theme tune to a film of that name in 1967?

49. Which three-suite work was composed by Handel and first performed in 1717 after King George I had requested a concert on the River Thames?

50. In which city was *Carmina Burana* by Carl Orff first staged in 1937?

Answers

1. Nicholas Lanier
2. Trombones
3. Napoleon Bonaparte
4. Royal Military School of Music
5. 'Pathetique'
6. Aldeburgh
7. Baroque
8. Elgar
9. Worcester
10. Deafness
11. Vivaldi
12. *Rockaria*, ELO
13. Harrison Birtwhistle
14. Chamber music
15. Gorecki
16. Rough, imperfect pearl
17. Staircase
18. Smetana
19. Mandolin
20. USA
21. Rodrigo
22. Castrati
23. Handel
24. *Monty Python's Flying Circus*
25. Tchaikovsky
26. Wagner
27. Manchester
28. Dvorak
29. *Dictionary of Music and Musicians*
30. The Russian revolution
31. Motet
32. 1824
33. Ralph Vaughan Williams
34. Thomas Beecham

35. Felix Mendelssohn
36. *I Believe In Father Christmas*, Greg Lake
37. The Last Post
38. Purcell
39. W.H. Auden
40. Herbert von Karajan
41. Train wreck
42. Marion Stein
43. The National Gallery
44. Ludwig II
45. Balalaika
46. Sturm und Drang
47. Gamelan
48. Elvira Madigan
49. *Water Music*
50. Frankfurt

Operas

Who wrote the following operas or operettas?

1. *Faust*
2. *Carmen*
3. *Lucia di Lammermoor*
4. *Rigoletto*
5. *The Barber of Seville*
6. *Tosca*
7. *Tristan und Isolde*
8. *Turandot*
9. *I Pagliacci*
10. *The Marriage of Figaro*
11. *Cavalleria Rusticana*
12. *Boris Godunov*
13. *Hansel und Gretel*
14. *The Mask of Orpheus*
15. *Oedipus Rex*
16. *Prince Igor*
17. *Bluebeard's Castle*
18. *Eugene Onegin*
19. *Acis and Galatea*
20. *La Belle Helene*

Answers

1. Charles-Francois Gounod
2. Georges Bizet
3. Gaetano Donizetti
4. Giuseppe Verdi
5. Gioachino Rossini
6. Giacomo Puccini

7. Richard Wagner
8. Ferruccio Busoni
9. Ruggiero Leoncavallo
10. Wolfgang Amadeus Mozart
11. Pietro Mascagni
12. Modeste Mussorgsky
13. Engelbert Humperdinck
14. Harrison Birtwistle
15. Igor Stravinsky
16. Alexander Borodin
17. Bela Bartok
18. Pyotr Ilyich Tchaikovsky
19. Georg Frideric Handel
20. Jacques Offenbach

Musicals

From which musicals do the following songs come?

1. *I Can't Say No; Out of my Dreams; People Will Say We're In Love*
2. *Get Me To the Church on Time; I Could Have Danced All Night; With a Little Bit of Luck*
3. *Feed the Birds; Let's Go Fly a Kite; A Spoonful of Sugar*
4. *How Long Has This Been Going On; My One and Only; S'Wonderful*
5. *True Love; Well Did You Evah; Who Wants To Be a Millionaire?*
6. *If I Loved You; June Is Busting Out All Over; Mister Snow*
7. *Summer Nights; Hopelessly Devoted To You; Greased Lightning*
8. *And This Is My Beloved; Baubles, Bangles and Beads; Stranger in Paradise*
9. *Anything You Can Do; Doin' What Comes Naturally; There's No Business Like Show Business*
10. *As Long As He Needs Me; Consider Yourself; I'd Do Anything*
11. *Be Careful, It's My Heart; Happy Holiday; White Christmas*
12. *Embraceable You; I Got Rhythm; I'll Build a Stairway to Paradise*
13. *I Get a Kick Out of You; You're the Top; What a Joy to Be Young*
14. *I Am What I Am; Song on the Sand; Look Over There*

15. *The Sun Has Got His Hat On; The Lambeth Walk; Leaning on a Lamp-Post*
16. *Over the Rainbow; Ding Dong! The Witch is Dead; If I Only Had a Brain*
17. *Ol' Man River; Can't Help Lovin' Dat Man; Dandies on Parade*
18. *Big Spender; If My Friends Could See Me Now; Too Many Tomorrows*
19. *Love Changes Everything; The First Man You Remember; Anything But Lonely*
20. *Tea For Two; I Want To Be Happy; I've Confessed to the Breeze*

Answers

1. *Oklahoma*
2. *My Fair Lady*
3. *Mary Poppins*
4. *Funny Face*
5. *High Society*
6. *Carousel*
7. *Grease*
8. *Kismet*
9. *Annie Get Your Gun*
10. *Oliver*
11. *Holiday Inn*
12. *An American in Paris*
13. *Anything Goes*
14. *La Cage Aux Folles*
15. *Me and my Girl*
16. *The Wizard of Oz*
17. *Show Boat*
18. *Sweet Charity*
19. *Aspects of Love*
20. *No, No, Nanette*

Tiebreakers

If you are playing with teams and a tie-breaker is required, the nearest correct answer to the following questions wins.

1. *The Mikado* was Gilbert & Sullivan's most successful collaboration. It had its first performance at the Savoy Theatre on 14 March 1885; for how many nights did the initial run last?
2. What is the official estimate for the number of people who attended the Live Aid concert at Wembley Stadium in July 1985?
3. Status Quo have had more UK Top 40 hits than any other group, the last to date being in 2010 (three of these were re-recordings of numbers that had already been Top 10 hits, one a live version, but these count as separate hits). How many were there altogether?
4. What is the official estimate for the numbers who attended Rod Stewart's New Year's Eve 1994 Concert at Copacabana, Rio de Janeiro?
5. How many UK No. 1 hits has Elvis Presley had altogether, including a remix credited to 'Elvis vs JXL' in 2002, but not counting the reissued singles in 2005 (which had previously been No. 1 hits the first time they were released)?
6. When Iron Maiden's *Bring Your Daughter to the Slaughter* entered the singles chart at No. 1 in January 1991, it had what had been the lowest first-week sale for a chart-topping single at the time – how many copies?

7. The week after he died in June 2009, Michael Jackson held the record for the most simultaneous hits in the UK Top 40 in any one week. How many altogether?
8. The week after he died in January 2016, how many albums did David Bowie have in the UK Top 20?
9. In February 2014 Queen's 'Greatest Hits' was confirmed as the all-time best-selling album in the UK, with estimated sales of how many copies?
10. 'South Pacific', the original soundtrack album, topped the UK album charts from the first chart in November 1958 to March 1960, and returned to the No. 1 spot later on in 1960 and 1961. How many non-consecutive weeks did it spend in pole position?

Answers

1. 672
2. 72,000
3. 57
4. 3,500,000
5. 18
6. 29,918
7. 13
8. 6
9. 6,000,000
10. 115

The author

John Van der Kiste has written over sixty books, including historical and royal biographies, works of local history, true crime, music, plays and fiction. He has reviewed records and books for various national, local and independent publications and websites, and is a contributor to the *Oxford Dictionary of National Biography*. He lives in Devon.

For a complete list of his other titles currently available, please visit Amazon.co.uk/Amazon.com

Printed in Great Britain
by Amazon